wallpaperPROJECTS

THE DESERT   LIFE NATURE LIBRARY

THE BODY

wallpaperPROJECTS

MORE THAN 50 CRAFT AND DESIGN IDEAS FOR YOUR HOME, FROM ACCENTS TO ART

DEREK FAGERSTROM *and* LAUREN SMITH

Photographs by Erin Kunkel

CHRONICLE BOOKS

SAN FRANCISCO

Library of Congress Cataloging-in-Publication Data:

Fagerstrom, Derek.
  Wallpaper projects : More than 50 craft and design ideas for your home, from accents to art / Derek Fagerstrom and Lauren Smith.
       p. cm.
  Includes index.
  ISBN: 978-0-8118-6706-1
1. Paper work. 2. Wallpaper. 3. Handicraft. I. Smith, Lauren. II. Title.

TT870.F32 2009

745.54—dc22

                                        2008035027

Manufactured in Singapore

A QUIRK PACKAGING BOOK

Designed by Lynne Yeamans and Bisou Creative
Edited by Lindsay Herman

10 9 8 7 6 5 4 3 2 1

Chronicle Books LLC
680 Second Street
San Francisco, California 94107

www.chroniclebooks.com

Acknowledgments

A HUGE, GIGANTIC THANKS to Christina Seely and Stacy Pancake for being so generous and supportive, and for allowing us to make an unbelievable mess in their homes and offices during the production of this book. Thanks also to Mike Chino, Jen Trolio, and Jason Randel for letting us invade their homes as well.

Aurora Crispin, Mike Chino, and Leigh Metcalf lent us their very capable hands on a number of these projects, and ran the show at our Shoppe when we were off wallpapering. They're the best helpers anyone could ever ask for.

Thanks to Claire Bigbie for letting us raid her treasure-filled prop closet, and to Lorena Siminovich for providing us with so many beautiful vintage wallpapers.

It hardly seems fair to take credit for a book when so many smart, thoughtful people held our hands at every step. Thanks so much to the very talented folks at Quirk Packaging: Sharyn Rosart, Lindsay Herman, Sarah Scheffel, Lynne Yeamans, and to the lovely Kate Prouty at Chronicle Books. Many thanks as well to Bisou Creative, our fantastic designer. Kate Lydon was instrumental in getting this project off the ground. We thank her for being such a wonderfully creative partner and friend.

We would never have even considered making a book had it not been for the inspiration and invaluable advice of our friends Todd Oldham and Vital Vayness. Thank you for all that you've given us.

We've been huge admirers of Lena Corwin for a long time now. It's a big thrill for us to have collaborated with her on a custom wallpaper design for this book. We thank her for contributing such creativity and enthusiasm to this project.

The most enjoyable part of this whole process has been the opportunity to spend so much time with our friend and favorite photographer, Erin Kunkel. Not only did she make everything look beautiful, but her patience, professionalism, and humor made all this work seem like one giant playdate.

Of course there would be no book at all were it not for the unbelievably talented and creative artists, designers, and distributors who continue making amazing patterns and papers year after year. Thank you not just for providing us with paper to play with, but inspiration to do so as well.

AS WITH ALL of our creative pursuits,

this book would not have been possible without the inspiration and encouragement

from our wonderful parents. Thank you so much Bev, Jim, Dick, and Linda.

WE LOVE YOU!

Contents

Chapter Three

Chapter Four

Introduction

Why Wallpaper?

This is an excellent question. The fact that you've picked up this book and made it this far probably means that you have a few answers of your own. Nevertheless, we thought we'd kick things off by sharing even more reasons why introducing wallpaper into your home and life is a particularly good idea right now.

It's beautiful.

Yes, this is certainly true. If you've spent any time browsing home décor books or magazines, or clicked around on any design blog worth its salt, you've undoubtedly noticed all the gorgeous contemporary and traditional wallpapers making their way back into the mainstream of interior design. Artists and designers of all stripes are not only rediscovering wallpaper, they're reinventing it. Aided by remarkable innovations in digital printing, design, and distribution, many manufacturers are exploding traditional expectations of what wallpaper can be, offering consumers all sorts of new and exciting options—from types of paper and ink to alternative eco-friendly materials to affordable custom designs.

It's versatile.

Sure, paint is great, but it's got nothing on wallpaper. Even with 101 different shades of white to choose from, painting a room can only get you so far. Wallpaper, on the other hand, can (and will) completely transform a space. Depending on what pattern, motif, or colorway you choose, applying wallpaper to even just a single accent wall can make a room feel tall, wide, small, big, bright, dark, fun, serious, quiet, loud, funky, classic...whatever look or mood you're going for, there is a perfect paper out there for you.

It's easy and fun.

Forget all your preconceived notions about wallpaper. It isn't messy, or hard to install. It's not some sort of interior design tattoo that you'll be stuck with forever. The papers and adhesives on the market today have made the whole process much safer and more forgiving, and the results more durable yet even easier to remove. If you make a good game plan and use the right tools (see Wallpaper 101 on page 14), we bet you'll be pleasantly surprised at how easy wallpapering actually is.

It's great on and off the wall.

Every wallpaper project is different, but one thing they all have in common is leftover scraps. With a bit of crafty ingenuity you can turn what would normally be inevitable waste into a unique opportunity to beautifully accent different areas in your home, create personalized stationery and accessories, revamp tired pieces of furniture, create frame-worthy works of art, make one-of-a-kind gifts...the options are endless. We've included more than 50 fun projects in this book to get your creative juices flowing.

A Very Brief History

It appears that people have been decorating their walls, well, ever since there have been people and walls—cave paintings in the south of France date back millennia. But when it comes to wallpaper, its origins can be traced to China, where the process for making paper was developed about 2,000 years ago. Wallpaper as a decorative trend didn't really take off until the fifteenth century when Europeans replaced the heavy, musty tapestries adorning their palace walls with hand-painted paper instead. Of course, not just anyone could afford these artfully rendered botanical, landscape, or battle scenes, and wallpaper quickly became a popular way to broadcast one's wealth and social status.

It wasn't until the advent of modern printing technology during the late eighteenth century that wallpaper began making its way into the homes of the middle and lower classes. While advances in manufacturing made it more affordable, it still had a few drawbacks. It quickly gained notoriety as the perfect breeding ground for all sorts of bacteria as well as armies of creepy crawlies that would make their homes behind the paper, emerging in the night to pay visits on unsuspecting homeowners. Viewed as an unsanitary health threat, wallpaper soon fell out of favor and, subsequently, fashion. Wallpaper didn't disappear entirely, of course, and every so often it would experience a renaissance, prompted by improvements in hygiene, or the enthusiasm of artists and designers, notably those in the Art Deco and Bauhaus schools.

World War II was the turning point in wallpaper's tumultuous history. The war inspired breakthroughs in a number of industries important in the development of contemporary wallpaper. Advancements in adhesives, plastics, textiles, and paints led directly to the creation of synthetic papers that were sanitary, durable, easy to use, and budget-friendly.

Many of us have our own personal histories with wallpaper, and oftentimes it isn't pretty. We're haunted by the tacky florals or psychedelic prints from the homes we grew up in during the 1960s and '70s. An interior design backlash was inevitable, and once the 1980s arrived, consumers retreated from pattern, preferring a safer, simpler look they could achieve with those 101 shades of white.

Today, a wonderful convergence of technology and artistry has made wallpaper an irresistible design option. It's a very exciting time to get back to wallpapering.

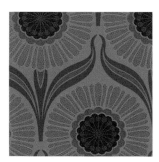  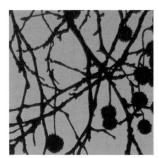 

chapterONE

WALLPAPER 101: TOP TO BOTTOM INSTRUCTIONS

ESSENTIAL TOOLS AND MATERIALS

Unlike some home decorating projects, wallpapering doesn't require a garage full of specialized or expensive tools and ingredients. The few things you do need are inexpensive, reusable, and should be readily available at your local hardware store.

Wallpapering Supplies

PLASTIC SHEETS AND DROP CLOTHS: Cover your work surface with plastic sheeting to prevent any paste from getting on your table. Drop cloths can be used to cover furniture, and should be placed along the bottom of the wall to catch any errant paste splatters.

BROAD KNIFE: A 4" broad knife (see Metric Conversion Chart on page 141) is a great tool for creasing paper into corners and cutting off excess paper. It can also come in handy when removing old wallpaper.

UTILITY KNIFE: It's very important that you can snap off and replace the blades of your knife. You don't want any tears or rips in your wallpaper, so change out the blade after every couple of cuts.

PENCIL: You'll need a good pencil for a number of important tasks: drawing out your room schematic, outlining measurements on wallpaper for smaller craft projects, taking notes, making calculations, numbering your wallpaper strips, and drawing your plumb lines.

LEVEL: Use a level to draw straight vertical lines on your wall that'll help align your paper. Choose a model that will give you a level reading both vertically and horizontally. They come in many different lengths, so be sure to get one you can easily handle. Remember that the longer the level, the fewer times you'll need to reposition it on the wall while drawing your plumb line.

PAINT ROLLER AND TRAY: If you're papering a large surface, a paint roller is a great way to apply wallpaper paste to your paper or the wall. Use a roller with a low nap or foam cover.

WALLPAPER BRUSHES: As an alternative to the paint roller, a stiff-bristled **pasting brush** can also be used to apply an even layer of paste to the back of your paper. You'll be using this a lot, so make sure to get one that fits comfortably in your hand. A stiff-bristled **smoothing brush** is used to smooth the pasted paper onto your wall. The bristles work magic on bubbles and will help the paper adhere securely to the surface.

PLASTIC FLOAT: This tool, normally used for plastering, adds the finishing touch to pasted paper by reducing air bubbles, evenly distributing paste beneath the paper, and smoothing down seams.

BUCKET AND SPONGE: Once the paper is up on a wall, you'll need a damp sponge to wipe away any excess paste from seams and the front surface of your paper.

Craft Supplies

Check around your house for some basic craft tools that will come in handy on a wallpaper craft project. And since the projects in this book range from small-scale crafts to big-time home décor, it's always a good idea to take a look at the required tools for each one before you begin. Your cute wallpaper magnets will require a few different supplies from your window shades (like, say, magnets), so it's best to be prepared at the start.

X-ACTO KNIFE: Use an X-Acto to create precise cuts in all types of paper. Be sure to always have extra blades on hand.

METAL RULER: If you plan on cutting paper with a blade, you need a metal ruler. Run the blade along the ruler's edge and you'll get a straight, clean cut every time.

CUTTING MAT: Protect your work surface by using a self-healing cutting mat every time you make a cut.

BONE FOLDER: For clean folds and creases, use a bone folder to first score your paper and then fold.

HOLE PUNCH: Very useful for making holes (obviously), hole punches can also be used to add decorative touches to all sorts of paper projects.

ROUNDED-CORNER PUNCH: We're not sure if there's a scientific explanation for this, but rounded corners always look better than straight ones.

MOD PODGE: An incredibly versatile adhesive perfect for all types of paper crafts, Mod Podge dries clear, so it also works wonders as a protective sealant.

RUBBER CEMENT: Anytime you glue one piece of paper to another, this is the way to go. When using rubber cement, brush it onto both surfaces and let dry slightly before adhering.

SPRAY ADHESIVE: This is an effective method for covering large surface areas with adhesive. Just be sure to use it in a well-ventilated area, with no wind. As a general rule, when applying paper to an object, spray the back of the paper, not the object. Always give the adhesive a minute or two to set before adhering.

TACKY GLUE: A great all-purpose adhesive, tacky glue is useful for all manners of craft projects, paper or otherwise.

WALLPAPER OPTIONS

Unless you're using paper unearthed from Grandma's basement or purchased from a source that specializes in vintage or historic materials, the wallcoverings you'll find on the market today are either vinyl-coated or silk-screened on paper. Whether the paper is vintage fabric-backed, vinyl-coated, or a brand-new organic like cork or grass, always be sure to read any instructions included with the roll. Different manufacturers may have specific requirements for their papers.

VINYL-COATED: This wallpaper sports a protective vinyl coating, which makes the paper extra durable, scrubbable, and generally easier to maintain.

HAND SILK-SCREENED: These papers are carefully printed by hand using large screens. Some manufacturers coat their papers in a water-based glaze, which will allow you to clean them with a damp sponge. As concerns about the environment and toxic chemicals in the home have grown, more and more companies have begun to offer wallpapers printed on recycled paper using soy-based inks.

PREPASTED: Prepasting was big in the 1970s, and many manufacturers continue to produce papers with the adhesive already applied. Simply soak the rolls in water for a specified amount of time to activate the paste and then smooth the strips onto your wall.

FABRIC-BACKED: With a mesh-like woven fabric back, this type of wallpaper is extra durable and most commonly used in high-traffic or commercial settings.

Wallpaper Adhesives

Choosing the proper adhesive depends on the paper you are using. Always read the manufacturer's suggested installation instructions before you dive into a project. Today, adhesives generally fall into one of two categories—synthetic or organic.

SYNTHETIC: As you can imagine, synthetic adhesives contain chemicals, which make for a strong and durable bond. Using a synthetic adhesive also means you'll have a heck of a time getting it out of your carpet or off your dining room table should things get a bit messy. You should consider this type of adhesive if you're papering a wall in a very humid or high-traffic area, where the paper may need to withstand some extreme weather or serious wear and tear.

ORGANIC: In general, we recommend choosing an organic, water-soluble paste for most wallpaper projects. These starch-based adhesives are reliable and forgiving, won't stain or soil your workspace, and are easily strippable if you decide to tear down your wallpaper a year from now.

THE BIG COVER UP: Prepping Your Walls for Paper

Wallpapering is like cooking—everything will be much easier (and you're less likely to get burned) if you take the time to be properly prepared before you start. With all the planning and measuring, there will be a lot of numbers flying around, so we recommend you write everything down in an organized manner. Gather up all the necessary tools and ingredients (see pages 14–15) and organize them in your workspace. And speaking of a space, it doesn't take much—a long surface, like a dining room table, is pretty much all you'll need, especially if you "book" your paper. "Book your paper?!" Yes! Keep reading.

Take an Overview

The first step in planning your layout is to make a schematic drawing of the room, noting the location of windows, doors, and any other potential obstacles. When deciding where to hang the first strip, always keep the width of your wallpaper in mind. This will help you get a sense of where each strip will land once you start pasting them up on the wall. If you are doing a single wall, it's much better to start in a spot that will allow at least a 5" strip of wallpaper on either end of the wall. For whole-room installations, make sure to have your last piece land in a "dead" corner—somewhere inconspicuous where it won't be obvious if your pattern doesn't match up—like in a corner by a closet, or behind a door.

Once you've got an idea of the layout, give each strip of paper a number and mark that on your drawing. This will remove any guesswork later on, so you don't find yourself standing on a ladder with a wet piece of wallpaper in your hands, wishing you had planned this out better.

Calculate the Paper

This is probably the most difficult part of wallpapering, but only because it involves some very basic math skills. The most straightforward way to determine how much paper you will need is to measure the length of the wall (or walls) and multiply that by the height of the room.

Then find out how much comes in a roll of the paper you are interested in. Papers vary from around 20" to 27" wide, with the standard length of a single roll being 15' (double rolls are twice as long, obviously). Make your calculations, without subtracting any paper for windows or doors, and then add an extra roll just to be safe. You'll be glad to have extra paper for any unforeseen mishaps (our mantra: measure twice, cut once!), future patch jobs, or better yet, wallpaper crafts!

(continued)

Prepare the Room

In order to paper your walls, you're going to need access to them. Which means either moving furniture out or piling it up in the middle or opposite side of the room. Wallpapering is not a terrifically messy activity, but if you're worried about your furniture, throw a drop cloth over it. Prepping the walls actually kicks up the most dust, so now is a good time to place drop cloths at the foot of any walls you'll be papering.

Before any paper goes up, many things must come down. Start by removing all artwork and shelving. Wallpaper loves smooth surfaces: Keep an eye out for bumps or holes in the wall—they'll need to be sanded and spackled. Remove outlet covers, faceplates, and any other fixtures that will come down. Once you've got a nice blank slate, give it a good cleaning with a damp sponge. Wallpaper loves clean surfaces, too.

GETTING THE HANG OF IT: Applying Paper to Your Walls

Now that you've done all the necessary prep work, it's time to get to the fun stuff. Two sets of hands are better than one when it comes to handling long expanses of wet paper, so it's a good idea to invite over a friendly helper.

Cutting

This isn't the first time we've said it, and it may not be the last, but "Measure twice, cut once" is our rule when preparing to paper a room. Once you've drawn up your detailed schematic, measured your walls, and prepped your room, it's time to start cutting.

The rule to remember here is "height + 4"." The "height" of the wall plus 4" will ensure that you have an extra 2" on the top and 2" on the bottom of every strip. If the pattern of your paper is a straight match,

once you've cut your first piece you can simply line up the following pieces and make the same cut. If you have a drop match (when the pattern match requires shifting a strip up or down rather than straight across), make sure to line up each following piece so that the pattern matches before you make your cuts.

Always use a metal straight edge, like a ruler or carpenter's square, and make sure your utility knife has snap-off blades, which should be changed not just occasionally or frequently, but obsessively—after every few cuts. This is especially true later, when cutting off the excess from the wall.

After you've cut each piece, lightly number it on the back with a pencil according to your schematic drawing so you can keep track of your work.

Pasting

It's unfortunate that we don't have a catchy mantra when it comes to pasting your paper (we're working on it), because there are a couple important things to keep in mind. First, read the instructions that came with your paper. Different manufacturers may recommend different methods for installation. Prepasted papers, for example, just require a quick soak in water. But in general, the following instructions pertain to most situations. Cover your table with a plastic drop cloth and have all your tools within easy reach. Then, start pasting.

Materials

WALLPAPER

Tools

DROP CLOTH
WALLPAPER PASTE
WALLPAPER BRUSH
    OR PAINT ROLLER
PAINT TRAY

How-To

1. Lay your wallpaper strips on top of one another, pattern-side down, with the first piece on top of the pile. (When you spread the paste over the edges of the top piece, it'll go directly onto the back of the next piece, which means less mess and no wasted paste.)

2. Pour a nice, big glob of paste into a paint tray.

3. Use either a wallpaper brush or a paint roller to apply an even layer of paste to the entire back of the paper, working from the center out to the sides. It's especially important to make sure you get the edges, which will prevent your seams from showing. Because nobody wants their seams showing, right?

Booking

Once you have full paste coverage on your strip, it's time to book it. "Booking" your paper involves laying pasted sides together—which seems quite counterintuitive but ends up saving you space and ensuring better adhesion of your wallpaper. This process will allow the paste to activate and be properly absorbed by the paper. Rest assured, it will pull apart just fine.

How-To

1. With your first strip pasted-side up, grab one end and bring it toward the center of the strip, creating a very loose fold. Without creasing the paper, place the end down so the pasted sides are together.

2. Bring the other end toward the center and place it so that the cut lines are butting—thereby essentially folding your strip into thirds.

3. Now you can fold the strip onto itself a few times (no creases!) and set it aside while you paste up the next one. You can leave booked pieces in a plastic bag for up to half an hour without any problems. We generally paste and book 4 to 5 pieces at a time.

Hanging It Up

This is it. The moment of truth—applying the pasted paper to your wall. This is also when you discover wallpapering is much easier than you imagined it would be. The paper is totally manageable, the paste surprisingly forgiving....Congratulations, you are minutes away from enjoying a magically transformed room!

Materials

WALLPAPER (PASTED
    AND BOOKED)
PLASTIC BAG

Tools

DROP CLOTH
STEPLADDER
LEVEL
PENCIL
MEASURING TAPE
SMOOTHING BRUSH
PLASTIC FLOAT
SPONGE AND BUCKET
    OF WATER
4" BROAD KNIFE
UTILITY KNIFE WITH
    SNAP-OFF BLADES

How-To

1. Use a level and a pencil to lightly mark a plumb (perfectly vertical) line on your wall where you want to put up the first piece of wallpaper.

2. Unfold the top half of your first pasted-and-booked strip and, beginning at the top of the wall, line its edge up with your plumb line. Remember to keep that extra 2" on top (see Cutting on page 18).

3. As you line up the edge, press the paper against the wall and begin smoothing it down with your smoothing brush.

4. Once you reach the middle of the wall, unfold the bottom half of the paper and continue lining up the edge with the plumb line, smoothing as you go. You may notice a few small air bubbles, but don't panic—those will disappear as the paper dries. If there are a number of large air bubbles that are making you nervous, gently pull the paper away from the wall and smooth it down again.

5. With the paper in place, nice and straight, smooth the entire strip down with your brush, working from the center outwards.

6. Repeat the same smoothing process with your plastic float. This will spread the underlying paste evenly out toward the edge of the paper and press your seams flush to the wall.

7. Grab your second pasted strip and repeat steps 2 through 6. But instead of lining up the edge with the plumb line, you're now matching the pattern of the wallpaper.

8. Once you've got a few pieces up, gently wipe down the paper with a damp sponge, especially at the seams, to remove any paste that may have made its way out onto the front.

9. Continue pasting up your strips until you reach the end of the wall. If you're doing more than one wall, see page 22 for instructions on turning a corner.

10. Place your 4" broad knife at the top of the wall where it intersects with the ceiling or molding. Carefully slide the blade of your utility knife along the edge of the broad knife to create a clean, straight cut. Continue cutting in this manner until you've reached the end of the strip. Snap yourself off a fresh blade and move onto the next strip.

11. Repeat the same cutting process along the bottom edge of the paper where it intersects with the floor or molding.

And there you have it. An entire room transformed!

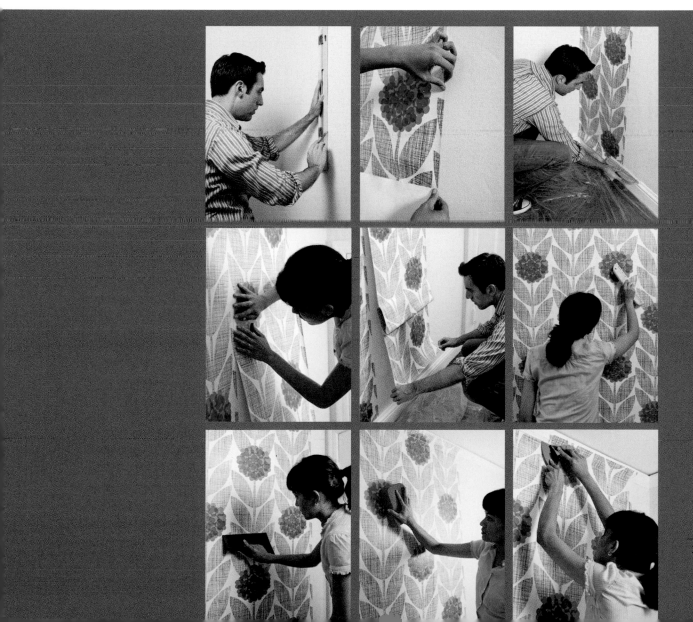

THE INS, OUTS, AND AROUNDS OF CORNERS

You've measured twice, cut once. You've mastered the art of pasting. The strips are going up straight and smooth. The whole process seems much easier than you expected. Everything is coming together, um, seamlessly, and just when you're about to take a breath and congratulate yourself, there it is...the corner.

Not to worry, the process for going in, out, or around corners is completely painless, and doing it properly takes only a few additional steps.

In and Out

The most common situation you'll encounter requires pasting the paper into, and then out of, a corner. It may look daunting, but with a few extra cuts and some minor calculations, you'll be on your way.

Tools

MEASURING TAPE OR RULER
PENCIL
UTILITY KNIFE
WALLPAPER PASTE AND BRUSH
PLASTIC FLOAT
4" BROAD KNIFE

How-To

1. Since you made a schematic of the room, your last full sheet is up, and you've got at least 5" of blank wall between the edge of the paper and the corner. Measure that distance, add ½", and cut your next strip to that width.

2. Paste this piece up just as you have been doing, matching up the seam with your last strip and smoothing it down against the wall. Use the edge of your plastic float to carefully crease the paper into the corner, and smooth the ½" piece onto the new wall.

3. Using your broad knife as a guide, trim off the 2" excess paper at the top and bottom of the wall. To help ease the paper into the turn, first make two vertical cuts, one at the top and the other at the bottom, right where the wallpaper meets the corner.

4. Now go back to the remainder of the piece you just cut and measure its width. Measure that same distance out from the corner on the uncovered wall and draw a plumb line.

5. Paste your strip, line its edge up with your plumb line, and smooth it onto the wall, right into the corner, overlapping the ½" of the previous strip. The reason for doing it this way is that the corners of a room are rarely, if ever, perfectly straight. By creating and working from a plumb line you can be sure the rest of your strips will go up nice and straight. Sure, your pattern will not match up perfectly, but you will be the only person able to spot this minor irregularity. It'll be our little secret.

Around

Occasionally, you may find it necessary to wallpaper around a corner. The process is similar to the inside corner technique with one special twist thrown in: the double cut.

Tools

MEASURING TAPE
   OR RULER
PENCIL
WALLPAPER PASTE
   AND BRUSH
UTILITY KNIFE

How-To

1. As before, your last strip on the first wall should end at least 5" before the corner. Take the width of your wallpaper strip and subtract ½".

2. Measure that distance from the edge of your last strip around the corner and mark that spot with a plumb line.

3. Hang your pasted paper by lining up the edge with the plumb line on the new wall.

4. Smooth the paper back around the corner toward your last strip, making cuts in the top and bottom excess paper to help turn the corner. Once you've smoothed the paper it should overlap your last strip by ½".

The Double Cut

When a wall isn't perfectly straight, or you've turned an outside corner, you may find instances where the seam of one strip of paper conspicuously overlaps another. The double cut is a great technique for turning this unsightly overlap into a perfectly tight seam.

Tools

RULER OR
   STRAIGHT EDGE
UTILITY KNIFE

How-To

1. Use a ruler and your utility knife to make a cut through both layers of paper directly down the middle of the overlap.

2. Pull off the separated top piece, then gently peel back the top of the overlapping piece just enough so you can remove the bottom layer of paper.

3. Then smooth back the overlap so that it butts directly against the edge of the previous paper. Voilà! No overlap and a nice tight seam.

REMOVING WALLPAPER

There are a number of ways to effectively remove wallpaper, and choosing the right one depends on a number of different factors, including how long the paper has been up, the type of paper, the adhesive that was used, and the surface of the wall. Fortunately, many of today's "strippable" adhesives and papers are designed for simple removal. As a general rule, it's best to start with the simplest technique, and if that doesn't work, move on to one of the more involved methods.

LIFT AND PEEL: Use your broad knife to peel up a corner or a seam of the paper and give it a tug. You might get lucky and the paper may come off in large strips simply by gently scraping and peeling it away.

PERFORATE AND SPRAY: If your paper isn't cooperating by peeling off in sizeable strips, the next option is to attack it with a paper tiger. This handy tool, available at most hardware stores, has little rotary blades that take bites as they are dragged across the surface of the paper. By running this tool all over the wall you can create small perforations that will allow moisture to reach the adhesive. Once you've gone over the wall with the paper tiger, mist the paper with water. Give it a few minutes to break down the adhesive and then try scraping the paper off with your broad knife.

CHEMICALS AND STEAM: If the paper is still being stubborn, you may need to resort to more drastic measures. Manufacturers sell a variety of gels and solutions made specifically to remove wallpaper. Ask for a recommendation at your local hardware store, and make sure to let them know what kind of wall the paper is on. They may have different suggestions based on whether you've got drywall versus plaster. You'll still need to perforate, then either apply a gel or use a steamer filled with a chemical solution to remove the paper.

Temporary Installation

Lauan (pronounced "loo-on") is a very inexpensive, lightweight plywood that is a great option for temporary installations and for renters with landlords who won't permit more than a coat or two of paint on the walls. Simply measure your walls and get a few sheets of lauan cut to fit at your local lumberyard. Attach them to your walls with screws and apply your wallpaper as you would onto virgin walls. The paper will look great, and the whole installation can be removed in minutes leaving only a few holes to spackle.

chapterTWO

STYLISH CRAFTS USING WALLPAPER SCRAPS

Note Cards and Envelope Liners

MAKE AND SEND YOUR VERY OWN LINE OF STATIONERY.

There are a lot of great greeting cards out there, but no matter how fancy, cute, or clever they are, they just can't beat one that's handmade. And you don't have to be an artist or designer to create something memorable—the simple act of making elevates even the most basic card to something truly special.

Materials

BLANK CARDSTOCK

WALLPAPER SCRAPS
   (ONE 9" X 12" PIECE PER
   CARD AND ENVELOPE)

BLANK ENVELOPES

SCRAP PAPER FOR TEMPLATE

Tools

X-ACTO KNIFE

METAL RULER

PENCIL

RUBBER CEMENT

How-To

1. Cut the cardstock to a size that will easily fit inside your envelope when folded in half. Measure the dimensions, and then fold in half to make a note card.

2. Subtract ⅛" from all sides, and then draw these measurements on the back of your wallpaper. Cut out the rectangle.

3. Apply rubber cement on both the outside of the card and the back side of the wallpaper. Then center the wallpaper rectangle onto the unfolded card.

4. Fold the card and place it under a heavy object while the glue sets.

5. Create a template for the liner by opening the flap of an envelope and tracing its entire perimeter onto a piece of scrap paper.

6. Subtract ⅛" from all sides, and cut out the template.

7. Place the template over your wallpaper and cut around it.

8. Apply rubber cement on both the inside of the envelope and the back side of the wallpaper. Then carefully slide the paper into place.

9. Set the envelope under something heavy while the glue sets.

Journal Covers

COLLECT YOUR THOUGHTS IN A SET OF CUSTOM JOURNALS.

We are list makers. Whether it stems from our obsession with organization or our penchant for procrastination, it's hard to say. But all those lists need homes. And we've found that even the most mundane list takes on special significance when it's been jotted down in a delightful notebook.

Materials

BLANK SOFTBOUND JOURNAL
WALLPAPER SCRAPS
¼"-WIDE ELASTIC

Tools

PENCIL
SCISSORS
RUBBER CEMENT
RULER
SMALL HOLE PUNCH
CLEAR NAIL POLISH
   (OPTIONAL)
GROMMET PUNCH WITH
   GROMMETS

How-To

1. Open the journal and lay it flat on the back side of your wallpaper.

2. Trace around the edges with a pencil.

3. Cut out the wallpaper cover with scissors.

4. Apply an even layer of rubber cement to both the covers of the journal and the back side of the wallpaper cover.

5. Carefully line up the edges of the paper and the journal and press down firmly.

6. For an elastic book band, cut a strip of elastic that is 2" longer than the height of the journal.

7. Punch holes ¼" from the top and bottom of the back cover.

8. Cut a small hole in the elastic band where you will be inserting the grommet. To prevent fraying, you may want to dab a little clear nail polish on the ends of the band.

9. Line up the hole in the band over the punched hole in the cover and insert a grommet (with the lip on the outside) through all layers.

10. Squeeze together using a grommet punch.

11. Repeat with the other end of elastic band.

Tip

You can line the inside covers of the journal with more wallpaper using the same technique used for the outer covers.

Bookmarks

USE A PRETTY PAPER MARKER, AND NEVER LOSE YOUR PLACE AGAIN.

It's true that you can use pretty much any old thing to hold your place in a book. Receipts, boarding passes, and business cards will all get the job done. But we think a pastime as pleasurable as reading deserves something a little special, like a custom set of bookmarks made from wallpaper trimmings.

Materials

WALLPAPER SCRAPS
6" STRAND OF YARN

Tools

RULER
PENCIL
SCISSORS
DECORATIVE-EDGE CRAFT
    SCISSORS (OPTIONAL)
SMALL HOLE PUNCH

How-To

1. Cut out a 1½" x 8" piece of wallpaper with scissors.

2. For added flair, cut along the long edges with decorative-edge craft scissors.

3. Punch a small hole in the center of the top of your bookmark.

4. Thread the yarn through the hole, and secure it with a slipknot.

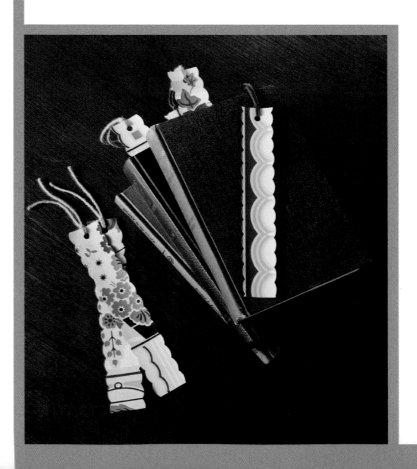

Paperweight

MAGNIFY A FAVORITE PATTERN WITH THIS HANDY LITTLE HELPER.

Using a traditional glass-domed paperweight is certainly useful when working with wallpaper, and it's also a great way to add a touch of class to an otherwise unruly desk.

Materials

GLASS DOME KIT (AVAILABLE AT
    OFFICE SUPPLY STORES OR
    ONLINE)
WALLPAPER SCRAP

Tools

PENCIL
SCISSORS

How-To

1. Glass dome kits generally come with a dome, a backing, and an adhesive felt bottom piece. Position the backing over your wallpaper and lightly trace around it with a pencil.

2. Cut out the circle with scissors and place it right-side up in the dome's interior lip.

3. Remove the backing from the felt bottom piece and adhere it to the bottom of the dome.

Binder Covers and Tin Can Pencil Holder

COORDINATE YOUR WORKSPACE WITH CUSTOM-MADE ACCESSORIES.

With just a few scraps of wallpaper you can take a mixed-up mess of a desk and pull it all together by color or theme. Tin cans wrapped in different colorways and ordinary binders covered in matching papers make for an organized and ogle-worthy space.

BINDER COVERS

Materials

BINDER WITH CLEAR COVERS
WALLPAPER SCRAPS
    (ONE 20" × 12" PIECE PER BINDER)

Tools

METAL RULER
PENCIL
X-ACTO KNIFE

How-To

1. Measure the clear front, back, and side pockets of the binder.

2. Transfer the measurements to the back side of your wallpaper, and cut the pieces to size using an X-Acto knife and metal ruler as your guide. Gently slide them into the binder pockets.

3. To create a continuous scene across the spines of adjacent binders, cut the spine pieces from the same area of wallpaper and arrange the binders accordingly on a shelf.

PENCIL HOLDER

Materials

CAN
WALLPAPER SCRAP

Tools

MEASURING TAPE
PENCIL
X-ACTO KNIFE
METAL RULER
SPRAY ADHESIVE

How-To

1. Measure the height and circumference of the can, adding ½" to the circumference for overlap.

2. Transfer the measurements to your wallpaper, and cut the piece to size.

3. Apply an even amount of spray adhesive to the back side of your paper, and wrap it around the can, smoothing down the paper as you go.

Magnets

TURN YOUR FRIDGE INTO A CANVAS FOR CREATIVITY.

Kitchens are tough. Other than a fresh coat of paint and some cute dishware and accessories, it can be a hard place to make a decorative dent. Luckily, one of the most common appliances also makes for a wonderful blank slate for all kinds of peel-and-stick fun.

Materials

STICKY-BACKED MAGNETIC
    SHEETING (AVAILABLE AT
    CRAFT AND HARDWARE
    STORES)
WALLPAPER SCRAPS

Tools

FINE-TIPPED INDELIBLE MARKER
SCISSORS

How-To

1. Peel back the paper on the magnetic sheeting and adhere it to your wallpaper.

2. Photocopy or trace the teardrop template below onto the magnetic side of the sheeting with an indelible marker.

3. Cut out your designs with scissors.

4. Adhere your homemade magnets to the metal surface of your choice.

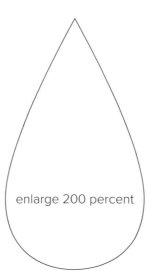

enlarge 200 percent

Magnet Board

AN ORGANIZATIONAL SYSTEM THAT YOU (AND EVERYTHING ELSE) CAN STICK TO.

Getting organized doesn't have to be a tedious chore. By creating an aesthetically pleasing system for keeping things tidy, you might even (dare we say?) enjoy the process. Covering a standard magnet board—accessories and all—in a great wallpaper can boost the fun-factor without sacrificing functionality.

Materials

MAGNET BOARD
WALLPAPER SCRAPS
MAGNETIC PENCIL CUPS

Tools

METAL RULER
PENCIL
X-ACTO KNIFE
SPRAY ADHESIVE

How-To

1. Measure the magnet board and draw these measurements on the back side of your wallpaper with a pencil.

2. Cut out the paper using an X-Acto knife and metal ruler as your guide.

3. Apply an even coat of spray adhesive to the back side of your paper, and adhere it to the front of the magnet board.

4. Measure the front and sides of the magnetic cups, adding a ½" allowance to wrap around the back.

5. Transfer the measurements to your wallpaper, cut out the paper, and adhere it to the cups using the same technique.

Tip

For some extra fun, choose a design element from the paper and create your own custom magnet. (See Magnets, page 37.)

Flower Brooch

GIVE NEW MEANING TO THE TERM "WALLFLOWER."

A homemade wallpaper brooch not only adds color and texture to any outfit, it's also a fun way to carry around a pretty little reminder of home. If it looks good on your walls, it'll look great on you.

Materials

WALLPAPER SCRAPS IN
   CONTRASTING PATTERNS
   (ONE 4" SQUARE OF EACH
   PATTERN PER BROOCH)
CLEAR CONTACT PAPER
½" BRAD
FLAT PINBACK

Tools

1" CIRCULAR CRAFT PUNCH
SMALL HOLE PUNCH
HOT GLUE GUN

How-To

1. Cover your wallpaper scraps with clear contact paper.

2. Punch out six circles of contrasting wallpaper (three of each color or pattern).

3. Arrange the circles into a flower shape by sliding one edge of each circle underneath the adjacent circle.

4. When you reach the final "petal," tuck it under the piece you started with.

5. Flip the flower over and secure the pieces together with a small strip of clear contact paper.

6. Punch a small hole in the center of the flower where the petals come together.

7. Insert the ½" brad through the hole and open its tabs.

8. Secure the tabs of the brad to the flat pinback with a line of hot glue.

Mini Badges

SPICE UP YOUR WARDROBE WITH DO-IT-YOURSELF ACCESSORIES.

Badge makers are so fun to use it's hard to decide whether they're tools or toys. Whichever it is, they are certainly addictive: Once you get going it's hard to stop—especially when there's plenty of wallpaper lying around. Look for interesting details to highlight on larger prints, or try making a collection of badges using different colorways of the same print.

Materials

CIRCLE TEMPLATE (FROM A CRAFT STORE, OR MADE FROM SCRAP PAPER)

WALLPAPER

Tools

PENCIL

SCISSORS

BADGE MAKER AND ACCESSORIES (SEE TIP)

How-To

1. Trace out appropriate-sized circles onto your wallpaper using a template. Since the edges of the circle will be crimped behind the badge, you can trace right onto the front side of the paper, which is helpful if you are making a specific crop in the design.

2. Cut out the badge designs with scissors from the sheet of wallpaper.

3. To make the badges, follow the instructions that came with your machine.

Tip

Badge makers come with all sorts of fun accessories. In addition to pins and buttons, you can make magnets and keychains using the same process. To find a badge maker, check your local craft or jewelry supply store, or www.badgeaminit.com.

Cuff Bracelet and Belt Buckle

WALLPAPER PRÊT-A-PORTER.

With so many amazing designs out there, don't be surprised when you find yourself wishing you could wear your wallpaper. It's normal. We're not saying you should wrap yourself like a mummy (or even like Diane von Furstenberg), but a visit to your local bead or jewelry store should provide you with all the materials you'll need to create your very own line of wearable wallpaper accessories.

Materials

CUFF BRACELET
BELT BUCKLE
WALLPAPER SCRAPS

Tools

MEASURING TAPE
PENCIL
SCISSORS
ROUNDED-CORNER PAPER
    PUNCH (OPTIONAL)
DOUBLE-SIDED TAPE

How-To

1. Measure the surface area of the cuff bracelet and/or buckle, and draw the measurements on the back side of your wallpaper.

2. Cut out your paper with scissors. You may want to cut it a hair smaller than the measurements so that a sliver of the metal will be visible around the edges. If necessary to fit inside the buckle's frame, round the corners of the paper with scissors or a rounded-corner punch tool.

3. Place double-sided tape on the back of the paper, and smooth it over the surface of the cuff and/or buckle. Make sure the tape is flush with the edge of the paper for a clean look.

Gift Tags

MAKE A SPECIAL GIFT SPECTACULAR WITH A ONE-OF-A-KIND TAG.

We love giving presents (getting them isn't so bad, either). A huge part of the thrill for us is coming up with fun and beautiful ways to wrap them up, and when it comes to wallpaper, you can make a whole holidays-worth of unique tags with just a few small scraps.

Materials

WALLPAPER SCRAPS

RIBBON OR STRING

SCRAP PAPER FOR BACKING
    (OPTIONAL)

Tools

GIFT TAG PUNCH (OPTIONAL)

PENCIL

SCISSORS

SMALL HOLE PUNCH

GLUE STICK (OPTIONAL)

How-To

1. If you have a gift tag punch (which can be purchased at most craft stores), creating gift tags is as easy as choosing your paper and punching them out. Otherwise, simply draw your tag shape onto the back of your wallpaper, or trace our luggage tag template on page 49, and cut it out with scissors.

2. Punch a small hole in the tag for the ribbon or string.

3. If the wallpaper is thin, adhere it to a thicker piece of paper with a glue stick to prevent it from curling.

Luggage Tags

SET YOUR BAG APART WITH AN IMPOSSIBLE-TO-MISS TAG.

We're paranoid about losing our luggage, so we always make sure it's labeled with up-to-date contact information. And when our bag finally does emerge on the baggage-claim carousel (hurray!), we want to spot it right away. Two great reasons to whip up a smart, one-of-a-kind luggage tag.

Materials

SCRAP PAPER FOR TEMPLATES
PAPER FOR CONTACT INFO
WALLPAPER SCRAPS
CLEAR CONTACT PAPER

Tools

PENCIL
SCISSORS
RUBBER CEMENT
SMALL HOLE PUNCH
BRAD

How-To

1. To create templates, photocopy or trace the tag templates below onto scrap paper, and cut them out with scissors.

2. Print or write your contact information on a separate sheet of paper, trace the tag template around it, and cut out the contact info tag for your backing piece.

3. Trace the templates onto your wallpaper of choice, then cut out your tag and strap.

4. Adhere the contact info sheet to the wallpaper with rubber cement.

5. Cover the front and back of your tag and strap with clear contact paper.

6. Punch a small hole in the top of the tag and at both ends of the strap.

7. Loop the strap and line up all three punched holes. Secure all layers together with a brad.

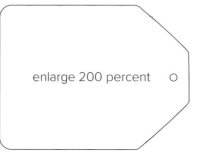

enlarge 200 percent   o

enlarge 200 percent

49

Portable Snack Tray

A GREAT-LOOKING TRAY MAKES ANY TREAT TWICE AS SWEET.

A portable place setting is a wonderful thing for incessant snackers like us. But this lovely tray could serve just as well as a place to stash art supplies, makeup, or anything else you like to keep close at hand.

Materials

SERVING TRAY

WALLPAPER SCRAP

CLEAR CONTACT PAPER
  (OPTIONAL)

Tools

METAL RULER

PENCIL

X-ACTO KNIFE

SPRAY ADHESIVE

BONE FOLDER

How-To

1. Measure the area of the tray, and transfer these measurements to the back side of your paper.

2. Cut out your rectangle with an X-Acto knife and metal ruler as your guide.

3. Apply an even layer of spray adhesive to the back side of your paper.

4. Carefully set the paper in place on your serving tray. Use a bone folder to smooth out the paper and press it into the corners.

5. If you'll be using the tray to transport food, you can seal it with a same-size piece of clear contact paper.

Swatch Watch

Try this project with **A.** a rich tapestry print, **B.** an artful graphic, or **C.** a bright op-art pattern. See Resources on page 142 for details.

A.

B.

C.

Party Pennants

GET THE PARTY STARTED WITH A STRING OF FESTIVE FLAGS.

From county fairs to Christmas tree lots, pennants have always been a clear indication that a good time is about to be had by all. But you don't need a national holiday—or any reason at all, for that matter—to create a celebratory mood. All you need is some string and a few fun scraps of wallpaper.

Materials

CARDSTOCK FOR TEMPLATE

WALLPAPER SCRAPS
(EACH AT LEAST 6" × 13")

STRING

Tools

PHOTOCOPIER

PENCIL

X-ACTO KNIFE

BONE FOLDER

METAL RULER

RUBBER CEMENT

How-To

1. Enlarge the diamond template 300 percent, so that it measures approximately 12" × 6" top to bottom.

2. Trace the pattern on a piece of cardstock, cut it out with an X-Acto knife, and use this as a template for the pennants.

3. Trace the template onto your wallpaper scraps of choice, and cut out your pennants.

4. Score a horizontal line across the middle of each paper with a bone folder and metal ruler as your guide, and fold it in half toward the back side.

5. Hang a pennant by folding it over the string and securing the front and back edges with rubber cement. Make sure you carefully line up all the edges.

6. Measure 3" down the string and attach the next pennant.

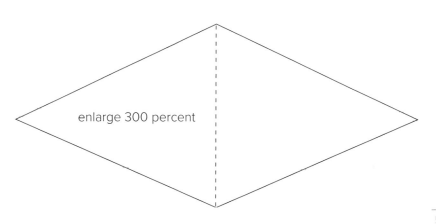

enlarge 300 percent

Pinwheels

CREATE A KINETIC SCULPTURE FOR YOUR HOME OR GARDEN.

Simple in design, timeless as a symbol of playfulness and innocence—pinwheels are an ideal way to display and enjoy every sort of bold and beautiful paper. We could watch them spin all day long.

Materials

WALLPAPER SCRAPS
   (5" SQUARE PER PINWHEEL)
3 BEADS
SMALL WOODEN DOWEL

Tools

METAL RULER
X-ACTO KNIFE
SMALL HOLE PUNCH
DREMEL (OR POWER DRILL
   WITH TINY BIT)
SMALL NAIL
HOT GLUE GUN

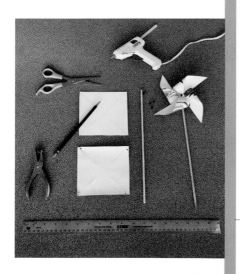

How-To

1. Cut out a 5" square piece of wallpaper.

2. Fold the square diagonally from corner to corner, unfold, and repeat on the opposite side to create an "x" fold across the paper.

3. Using an X-Acto knife and metal ruler as your guide, cut a 2" slit from the edge of each corner of the square, along the fold lines, creating eight corners total.

4. Punch a small hole at the tip of every other corner, and one through the center of the square.

5. Drill a small hole through the dowel about ¼" down from the top.

6. Insert a nail through the dowel, and slide a bead over the nail.

7. Pass the nail through the center hole from the back of the wallpaper.

8. Fold the punched tips toward the center of the square and slide them over the nail.

9. Slide the second bead over the nail.

10. Finally, place the last bead over the nail, securing it in place with a spot of hot glue.

Tip

If you don't have a dremel, try soaking the wooden dowel in water and pushing the nail through.

Paper Flowers

PICK YOURSELF A PRETTY (AND PERMANENT) BOUQUET

We love having fresh flowers around the house. It's one of the easiest and most pleasant ways to add fun colors and shapes to a room. With a few scraps of wallpaper you can fashion your own faux-floral arrangements in an endless variety of shapes, sizes, and colors. Best of all, these delightful daisies require no water and are always in season.

Materials

WALLPAPER SCRAPS
 (TWO 4" SQUARES
 PER FLOWER)
FLORAL WIRE (ONE 12"
 PIECE PER STEM)
DOT STICKERS
 (TWO PER FLOWER)
VASE (OPTIONAL)

Tools

TAPE (OPTIONAL)
PENCIL
SCISSORS
RUBBER CEMENT

How-To

1. Hold (or gently tape) two complementary scraps of wallpaper with back sides together.

2. Photocopy or trace the flower template below onto your wallpaper scraps.

3. Cut out your flower shapes with scissors, making sure not to mix up the matching front and back sides.

4. Cut the floral wire to an appropriate stem length.

5. Coat the backs of matching flowers with rubber cement.

6. Place the flower wire between the matching paper flowers and press them together.

7. Place a dot sticker at or near the center of the flower, on both the front and back.

8. Repeat for all flowers and arrange them in a nice vase or other container.

Accordion-page Photo Album

ADMIRE SPECIAL SNAPSHOTS IN AN ELEGANT FOLDING DISPLAY.

Whether you've inherited some family photos or are just looking for an excuse to print out those pictures clogging up your hard drive, an accordion-fold album is a great way to both store and display your prints.

Materials

HEAVY MAT BOARD
  (FOR COVERS)
WALLPAPER SCRAPS
20" × 30" SHEET OF
  HEAVY-DUTY PAPER
PHOTOS
PHOTO CORNERS

Tools

METAL RULER
X-ACTO KNIFE
PENCIL
RUBBER CEMENT
BONE FOLDER
CLEAR TAPE (OPTIONAL)

How-To

1. Using an X-Acto knife and metal ruler as your guide, cut out two pieces of heavy mat board that are at least ½" bigger than your photos on all sides. These are your album covers.

2. Cut out two pieces of wallpaper that are 1" bigger than your covers on all sides.

3. Center one of your mat board covers on the back side of one of the cut pieces of wallpaper and trace around it. Miter the corners at 45-degree angles, cutting to within ⅛" of the pencil marks to allow for the width of the mat board as you wrap the sides.

4. Apply rubber cement to the wallpaper and mat board, line up the mat board with the pencil outline, and press down on the board to adhere the pieces together.

5. Starting with the long sides, fold the wallpaper edges down toward the inside of the cover. Use your bone folder to press down the paper at the corners before repeating with the short sides. Repeat steps 3 to 5 with the other mat board cover.

6. For the accordion pages, cut a long strip of heavy-duty paper that measures ½" shorter than the wrapped cover (you will trim the width of the paper after it has been folded).

7. Measure the width of the cover and subtract ½". At this width, make your first fold in the paper. Press down into the fold with a bone folder. Continue folding accordion-style, until you have enough pages to accommodate your photos.

8. Trim off any excess paper. Alternatively, if you want to add pages, cut another length of paper and attach it with clear tape.

9. Attach the first and last pages of the album to the inside covers with rubber cement. Then add your photos using photo corners.

Cereal Box Magazine Holders

CREATE A CUSTOM LIBRARY FOR YOUR FAVORITE PERIODICALS.

We're big fans of magazines. In fact, we love them so much we sometimes have a hard time tossing them in the recycling bin. Having a dedicated and well-decorated spot for them makes us feel less guilty about keeping so many around.

Materials

EMPTY CEREAL BOX
  (APPROXIMATELY THE SAME
  SIZE AS YOUR MAGAZINES)
SCRAP PAPER FOR TEMPLATE
WALLPAPER SCRAPS

Tools

BLUE PAINTER'S TAPE
SCISSORS
PENCIL
X-ACTO KNIFE
BONE FOLDER
METAL RULER
RUBBER CEMENT
CLEAR TAPE

How-To

1. Determine how high you want the sides of your magazine holders to be, and mark the angles with blue tape on either side of the box. Cut off the top of the box with scissors, stopping at the tape line.

2. Create a template out of a large piece of scrap paper by tracing around the box and adding a 2" border all the way around. Miter the corners by making diagonal cuts in the 2" border that will allow you to fold the paper into the box in step 5.

3. Score along all fold lines with the tip of a bone folder and a ruler.

4. Apply rubber cement to the outside of the cereal box and the back side of the wallpaper.

5. Wrap the wallpaper around the box, folding all flaps inside the box and applying more glue where needed.

6. Wrap the bottom of the box like a present and secure with a strip of clear tape.

Tip

For an added bit of flair, line the interior of the box with a contrasting wallpaper or the same print in another colorway.

Covered Canisters

TRANSFORM AN OLD COOKIE TIN INTO A BEAUTIFUL ALL-PURPOSE CONTAINER.

Every year as the holidays approach, our relatives start sending us all sorts of edible delights in big metal tins. We gobble up the treats, but the tacky tins are a little harder to swallow. Giving them a wallpaper makeover makes them as pretty to look at as they are handy to have around.

Materials

COOKIE TIN

WALLPAPER SCRAPS

1 YARD OF ½"-WIDE
  GROSGRAIN RIBBON

Tools

MEASURING TAPE

RULER

PENCIL

SCISSORS

X-ACTO KNIFE

SPRAY ADHESIVE

TACKY GLUE

How-To

1. Measure the height and circumference of the cookie tin, adding ½" to the circumference for overlap.

2. Transfer the measurements to the wallpaper and cut out the piece with scissors or an X-Acto knife.

3. Place the lid top-side down on your paper and trace around it. Cut out the circle with scissors.

4. Apply an even layer of spray adhesive to the back side of your paper and carefully wrap it around the tin, smoothing down the paper as you go. Apply adhesive to the circle and press it onto the lid.

5. Measure the circumference of the lid and cut a piece of ribbon to length, adding 1" for overlap.

6. Apply tacky glue to the ribbon and wrap it around the edge of the lid. For a clean look, fold the raw edge of the ribbon under ½", dab it with glue, and press down.

Potato Leek Soup

4 potatoes, quartered
3 leeks
1/4 c. butter
1/2 c. milk
1/2 c. light cream
quart stock

Recipe Box

ORGANIZE CULINARY TIPS, TRICKS, AND HINTS IN ONE DELECTABLE BOX.

A stack of index cards and a few small pieces of wallpaper are all it takes to transform an otherwise ordinary box into a treasure trove of your family's favorite recipes.

Materials

RECIPE BOX
WALLPAPER SCRAPS
INDEX CARDS
CARDBOARD

Tools

MEASURING TAPE
METAL RULER
PENCIL
X-ACTO KNIFE
SPRAY ADHESIVE
RUBBER CEMENT

How-To

1. Measure the interior dimensions of the recipe box.

2. Transfer the measurements onto the back side of your wallpaper of choice. Cut out your pieces with an X-Acto knife, and line the box with the paper, using the technique for lining a box on page 81.

3. Create the recipe dividers by tracing around an index card onto a piece of cardboard. Draw staggered tabs on the tops of the dividers.

4. Adhere the wallpaper to the front sides of the cardboard by applying rubber cement on both the surface of the cardboard and the back of the wallpaper.

5. Cut out the dividers with an X-Acto knife.

6. Write your recipes on index cards and file them in your box.

Napkin Rings

PRETTY UP YOUR PLACE SETTINGS.

Regardless of what's being served, sitting down to a table decked out with cloth napkins always feels like a special event. Folding them up like pope hats or swans might be a bit much, but a simple ring covered in wallpaper is an easy way to elevate a meal—no origami skills required.

Materials

CARDBOARD PAPER-TOWEL
 TUBES
WALLPAPER SCRAPS

Tools

MEASURING TAPE
SCISSORS
PENCIL
DOUBLE-SIDED TAPE

How-To

1. Cut the length of a cardboard tube into 2" sections.

2. Measure the circumference of the cardboard tube, and add ½" for overlap.

3. Transfer the measurements on to the back side of your wallpaper, cut a piece to size, and adhere it to the tube with double-sided tape.

4. Repeat to make as many rings as you like.

Swatch Watch

Try this project with **A.** a bold graphic, **B.** a delicate floral, or **C.** an organic pastel.
See Resources on page 142 for details.

A.

B.

C.

Place Mats

MAKE EVERY MEAL MEMORABLE (AND LESS MESSY) WITH PERSONALIZED PLACE MATS.

A great meal is the sum of its parts. When we have guests for dinner, we certainly hope they'll enjoy the food, but as a little added insurance, we put a lot of thought into the presentation as well. We figure that if we dazzle them with the décor, perhaps they'll forget how flimsy the asparagus was. These place mats, in addition to protecting your table from stains and scratches, are a super-simple way to add color, texture, and personality to any meal.

Materials

WALLPAPER SCRAPS
(48" OF PAPER WILL MAKE
FOUR PLACE MATS)

Tools

METAL RULER

X-ACTO KNIFE

ROUNDED-CORNER PAPER
PUNCH OR SCISSORS

How-To

1. Using an X-Acto knife and metal ruler as your guide, measure and cut out four 12" x 17" rectangles of wallpaper.

2. Using a rounded-corner paper punch or scissors, round the corners of each place mat.

3. Bring the cut pieces to your local copy center for laminating. Most likely, they will be returned to you on one large sheet.

4. Carefully trim each place mat, ⅛" around the paper edge, with both your X-Acto knife and scissors, as necessary.

5. Round the corners of the plastic lamination as you did with the paper.

Swatch Watch

Try this project with **A.** a mod floral, **B.** a playful graphic, or **C.** an irreverent toile.
See Resources on page 142 for details.

A.

B.

C.

Alternate Paper Project: Coasters

The same process applies for coasters. Cut four 4" squares out of scrap wallpaper (we used contrasting colorways of the same print) and round the corners. Once they are laminated, you can use spray adhesive to mount them onto 4" squares of ⅛"-thick cork. Press under a heavy book overnight and let them dry completely before using.

Clock

A WONDERFUL EXCUSE TO KEEP YOUR EYE ON THE TIME.

A homemade clock is one of the more rewarding projects you can make with wallpaper scraps (i.e., it's much easier than it looks). By covering the face of even the simplest of shapes, you can create an utterly unique timepiece to perfectly complement any room in your house.

Materials

SCRAP PAPER FOR TEMPLATE
FOAM CORE
WALLPAPER SCRAPS
CLOCK MECHANISM
   (AVAILABLE AT CRAFT AND
   HARDWARE STORES)
CLOCK BATTERY

Tools

PENCIL
X-ACTO KNIFE
SPRAY ADHESIVE
SPRAY PAINT (FOR PAINTING
   CLOCK HANDS, OPTIONAL)
AWL OR SMALL
   SCREWDRIVER

How-To

1. Create a template for your clock by either enlarging our template on page 139, drawing a design by hand, or designing it on a computer.

2. Cut out your design with an X-Acto knife.

3. Trace your template on a piece of foam core and carefully cut around it using the X-Acto knife.

4. Apply an even layer of spray adhesive to the back of your wallpaper (see page 15 in Wallpaper 101 for more on this technique).

5. Lay your clock facedown on the paper and press evenly for a good bond.

6. If you'd like, spray paint the clock hands and set them aside to dry.

7. Flip the clock over, with the paper side down, and carefully cut around the edges with your X-Acto knife.

8. Lightly mark the spot where the clock hands will go, and use an awl or small screwdriver to punch through the board.

9. Insert the clock mechanism through the hole. You may need to create a few foam core "washers" (small squares of foam core with a hole in the middle that slip over the clock mechanism) to hold the pieces in place if your board isn't thick enough.

10. Put in a battery, set the time, and hang the clock up on a wall.

Lampshade

BRIGHTEN UP YOUR HOME WITH A CUSTOM WALLPAPER LAMPSHADE.

Lighting can make or break a space. Even the most tastefully decorated room can end up looking like a convenience store (or dive bar) if not properly lit. A few strategically placed floor and table lamps are a great way to wrangle your wattage, and wallpaper covers help tie everything together.

Materials

SCRAP PAPER FOR TEMPLATE
LAMPSHADE
WALLPAPER SCRAPS

Tools

PENCIL
RULER
SCISSORS
DOUBLE-SIDED TAPE

How-To

1. Create a template by placing a sheet of scrap paper on your work surface and setting the lampshade on its side on top of the paper.

2. Place the tip of your pencil just below the seam at the top of the shade, and slowly roll the lampshade over the paper, tracing on the paper as you go. Keep your pencil moving along with the shade as it arcs across the paper.

3. Once the shade has made a complete rotation, continue tracing ½" beyond the seam to create an overlap.

4. Set the shade back at the starting point and repeat the same process, this time with your pencil at the bottom seam of the shade.

5. Use a ruler to connect the ends of the arcs with straight lines.

6. Cut out your template with scissors and wrap it around your shade to test the fit.

7. Trace the template onto the back side of your wallpaper and carefully cut it out.

8. Wrap the paper around the shade and adhere it with a thin strip of double-sided tape along the ½" seam.

Picture Frame Mats

GIVE FRAMED ARTWORK AN EXTRA-SPECIAL EDGE.

Finding the right mat for a frame can be a frustrating and expensive endeavor. Making your own out of wallpaper is a quick and easy alternative that will save you money and make your artwork shine.

Materials

PICTURE FRAMES
CARDSTOCK (ACID-FREE,
   TO PREVENT YELLOWING)
WALLPAPER SCRAPS
ARTWORK

Tools

PENCIL
X-ACTO KNIFE
METAL RULER
SCISSORS
RUBBER CEMENT
BONE FOLDER
ARCHIVAL TAPE (ACID-FREE)

How-To

1. Remove the glass and backing from one of your picture frames and use either one as a template from which you will trace and cut out your mat from cardstock.

2. Determine the best width for your mat border. Using an X-Acto knife and metal ruler as your guide, cut out a rectangular window in the center of the cardstock, leaving an even border on all sides. Use this piece as a template to cut out mats for all your frames of this size.

3. Adhere one mat to the back side of a piece of wallpaper with rubber cement. Add 1" to all outer edges of the wallpaper, for folding over the mat's edges, and trim with scissors or an X-Acto knife.

4. Draw a rectangle on your wallpaper that is 1" smaller than the interior window of the mat, and cut it out.

5. Miter the outside corners of the wallpaper by cutting them off at 45-degree angles toward the outside corners of the mat.

6. Snip into the corners of the interior window and score along the edges with the tip of your bone folder and a metal ruler as your guide.

7. Apply rubber cement to the back side of your mat and fold down all remaining wallpaper flaps along the outside of the mat and the interior window.

8. Once the rubber cement has dried, attach the artwork to the mat using acid-free archival tape.

Display Box

HIGHLIGHT EVERYDAY OBJECTS ON A BEAUTIFUL BACKDROP.

Whether you're a collector of fine jewelry or just like to have a nice place to toss your pocket change, lining a simple box with brightly patterned paper is a great way to both organize and showcase your stuff.

Materials

JEWELRY BOX
WALLPAPER SCRAPS

Tools

METAL RULER
PENCIL
X-ACTO KNIFE
SPRAY ADHESIVE
BONE FOLDER

How-To

1. Measure the areas you will be covering with wallpaper.

2. Draw the measurements on the back side of your wallpaper. For our display box, we used two different papers with a similar color palette.

3. Using an X-Acto knife and metal ruler as your guide, cut out your wallpaper lining.

4. Apply an even layer of spray adhesive to the back of the wallpaper.

5. Carefully set the paper in place inside your box. Smooth it down with a bone folder and make sure it is pressed flat into the corners.

Swatch Watch

Try this project with **A.** a tonal geometric, **B.** a handprinted floral , or **C.** a modern stripe.
See Resources on page 142 for details.

A.
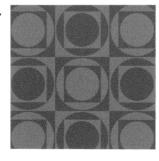

B.

C.

Wallet and Checkbook Cover

CUT AND STITCH POCKETBOOKS.

Who needs fabric? Both durable and versatile, reinforced scraps of wallpaper can be stitched together into the perfect place for stashing cash, checks, cards, or coins.

MINI WALLET

Materials

TWO WALLPAPER SCRAPS IN
    CONTRASTING PATTERNS,
    APPROXIMATELY 6" SQUARE
CLEAR CONTACT PAPER
THREAD

Tools

RULER
PENCIL
SCISSORS
SEWING MACHINE
SCALLOP-EDGE CRAFT SCISSORS

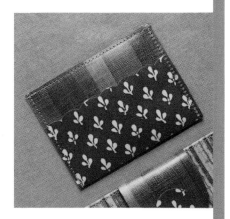

How-To

1. Measure and cut out a 4" x 5¾" rectangle from one scrap of wallpaper and cover both sides with clear contact paper. Trim the edges with scissors so the contact paper and wallpaper are flush. For a shortcut, photocopy or trace Mini Wallet A template on page 138 onto scrap paper, cut it out, and trace it onto your wallpaper.

2. Machine stitch along both short ends.

3. Cut a 4" square out of a contrasting piece of wallpaper, and cover both sides with contact paper. Trim the edges with scissors so the contact paper and wallpaper are flush.

4. Trim two opposite sides of the square with scallop-edge craft scissors. If you don't have scallop-edge scissors, photocopy or trace Mini Wallet B template on page 138 onto scrap paper, cut it out, and trace it onto your wallpaper.

5. Fold both pieces of wallpaper in half and place them together, aligned at their center folds, with the small piece on the outside.

6. Machine stitch up the side seams through all four layers, making sure to backstitch at the beginning and end to reinforce your seam.

CHECKBOOK COVER

Materials

WALLPAPER SCRAPS IN THREE
    PATTERNS
CLEAR CONTACT PAPER
THREAD
STICKY-BACKED VELCRO DOTS

Tools

RULER
PENCIL
SCISSORS
BONE FOLDER
SEWING MACHINE
1" INCH CIRCULAR HOLE
    PUNCH
DOUBLE-SIDED TAPE

How-To

1. Measure and cut out a 6½" × 13½" rectangle from one scrap of wallpaper, and cover both sides with clear contact paper. Trim the edges with scissors so the contact paper and wallpaper are flush.

2. Fold it in half with the short sides together, and crease with a bone folder.

3. Unfold the paper and place it on your work surface with the printed side down. Fold the short ends in toward the center, so the edges hit 1" away from the center crease.

4. For the tab closure, photocopy or trace the template on page 138. Trace your tab shape onto a scrap of contrasting wallpaper, cut it out, and cover it with contact paper.

5. Line up and center the cut edge of the tab along the outside folded edge of the large piece. Machine stitch through all layers.

6. Stitch along the edge of the fold on the opposite side, and then refold the entire piece in half along the center fold line.

7. Stitch up both sides, making sure to backstitch at the beginning and end to reinforce your seam.

8. Punch a 1" circle out of your third piece of wallpaper, and cover it with contact paper. Secure the circle to the outside of the tab with double-sided tape.

9. Remove the backing from both sides of a sticky-backed Velcro dot and press the Velcro sides together. Attach to the back side of your tab. Fold up the wallet and press down the tab, sticking the other side of the Velcro to the front side of the wallet.

Wine Crate Shadow Box

TURN A WINE SHOP CASTOFF INTO A MUSEUM-QUALITY DISPLAY CASE.

Over the years our various collections of tchotchkes, doo-dads, and baubles have taken over pretty much every nook and cranny in our home. Since ridding our home, and thus our lives, of our stuff was obviously out of the question, we decided we needed more nooks and crannies. A quick trip to our local wine shop provided us with the majority of the necessary raw materials (a wine crate) as well as a bottle of a little something with which to christen the project. We loved the rough-hewn look of the wooden box, and decided the (literal) branding on the sides only added to the charm. To contrast the raw wood, we chose a rich and elegant print we felt would elevate our *objets* to museum-worthy status.

Materials

WINE CRATE

WALLPAPER SCRAPS

Tools

METAL RULER

PENCIL

X-ACTO KNIFE

BONE FOLDER

SPRAY ADHESIVE

SAWTOOTH HANGER

HAMMER

NAILS

PEEL-AND-STICK RUBBER
     BUMPERS

HANGING HARDWARE

How-To

1. Use a ruler to measure the five interior walls of the crate.

2. Draw out the measurements in pencil on the back side of the wallpaper. Then, in order to avoid any potential gaps along the interior edges, add a 1" allowance as follows:

   • **Long pieces:** add 1" to each of the three sides that border the interior of the box.

   • **Short pieces:** add 1" allowance to the side that borders the back of the box.

   • **Back piece:** no allowance necessary

3. Use an X-Acto knife and metal ruler as your guide to carefully cut out the five pieces of paper.

4. Create fold lines by scoring along your pencil marks with a bone folder and a ruler as your guide.

5. Miter each of the interior corners by cutting a 45-degree angle from the outside edge in, along the 1" allowance.

(continued)

6. In a well-ventilated area, apply spray adhesive to the back sides of each of your long pieces. Carefully place them inside the box, lining up the folded edges with the edges of the box. Smooth out any air bubbles with the bone folder.

7. Next, spray and apply the short pieces. At this point, all four sides of the box will be lined, and the back will have a 1" border all the way around.

8. Spray and apply the back piece of paper to the box. Smooth out any air bubbles and let it dry completely before proceeding to the next step.

9. Decide which direction you want to hang your box, and attach a sawtooth hanger along the top edge using a hammer and nails. Apply peel-and-stick rubber bumpers along the bottom corners of the box to ensure that it hangs straight against the wall.

10. Mark the position of the box on the wall with a pencil, and attach it using the appropriate hanging hardware for your wall.

Swatch Watch

Try this project with **A.** a striking geometric, **B.** an elegant floral, or **C.** a refined graphic. See Resources on page 142 for details.

A.

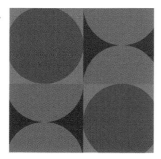

B.

C.

chapter THREE

DESIGNING WITH WALLPAPER

Bookshelf

LIVEN UP YOUR LIBRARY WITH A TOUCH OF PATTERN AND COLOR.

Some of our most prized possessions are books, and like all the meaningful objects in our home, they deserve an adoring display. A wallpaper backing will transform any old shelf into a dazzling backdrop for all your treasured tomes.

Materials

BOOKSHELF
WALLPAPER

Tools

MEASURING TAPE
PENCIL
UTILITY KNIFE
METAL RULER
SPRAY ADHESIVE
HAMMER AND BRADS
    (OPTIONAL)

How-To

1. Clear out your bookshelf and lay it flat on its back.

2. Measure the space between the shelves and cut your wallpaper to size using a utility knife and metal ruler as your guide.

3. Apply an even layer of spray adhesive to the back of your wallpaper and press firmly to the back of the shelf.

Tip

If your bookshelf has a detachable back, simply remove it and measure the entire piece. Cut your paper to size and apply it to the back. Reattach using a hammer and small brads.

Cabinet Recover

REVITALIZE A FLEA-MARKET FIND WITH A WALLPAPER MAKEOVER.

This forgotten office storage cubby was a sorry sight to behold. Freshened up with a quick coat of paint and a few feet of wallpaper, it's now the perfect place to store dishes, serving ware, or a couple bottles of our favorite cabernet.

Materials

CABINET

WALLPAPER

Tools

PAINT AND PAINTBRUSH
  (OPTIONAL)

MEASURING TAPE

METAL RULER

PENCIL

UTILITY KNIFE

SPRAY ADHESIVE

How-To

1. Paint any parts of the cabinet that need sprucing up and let it dry completely.

2. Remove handles from the doors and measure the width and height of each door. If you choose to wrap your paper around the sides of the doors, be sure to include the appropriate amount in your total measurement.

3. Trace the dimensions of the first door onto your wallpaper, and cut it out using a utility knife and metal ruler as your guide. If you'd like to match the pattern across the entire cabinet front, find the repeat on the roll and make sure it lines up with the first piece.

4. Trace and cut out the piece for your second door.

5. Apply an even layer of spray adhesive to the back side of your first piece of wallpaper, and press it onto the door. Repeat with the other piece, being careful to match up the pattern. If the pieces are big, you may want a second set of hands to help guide the paper smoothly onto the doors.

6. Reattach the door handles.

Tip

When working with spray adhesive, always make sure to get good coverage on the edges of the paper so they don't curl up after drying.

Glass-front Medicine Cabinet

DOCTOR UP YOUR MEDICINE CABINET WITH A VIBRANT WALLPAPER PATTERN.

No one wants visitors snooping in their medicine cabinet—but hey, if they're going to do it (and they are) you might as well give them something pretty to look at. Introducing color and pattern into this normally bland, antiseptic spot might even distract them from scrutinizing your personal stuff.

Materials

CABINET

WALLPAPER

Tools

MEASURING TAPE

PENCIL

X-ACTO KNIFE

METAL RULER

SPRAY ADHESIVE

How-To

1. Remove the shelves and measure the back and bottom of the cabinet.

2. Measure the tops, fronts, and bottoms of the shelves. Add up the total measurements for one piece of wallpaper that will wrap around each shelf.

3. Transfer your measurements onto the back side of your wallpaper, and cut out your pieces using an X-Acto knife and metal ruler as a guide.

4. Apply an even layer of spray adhesive to the back side of the wallpaper pieces and carefully line the back and bottom of the cabinet.

5. Apply adhesive to the shelf pieces and wrap them around the shelves.

6. Places the shelves back into the cabinet, and let them dry overnight.

Covered Stools

MAKE OVER A MODERN CLASSIC WITH COLOR.

Stools are great because they're simple, and maybe that's why we so often take them for granted. Lightweight, sturdy, stackable…there are a million reasons why they are one of the most versatile pieces of furniture you can buy. Add a bit of color and character to this classic design and they become as beautiful as they are useful.

Materials

WALLPAPER SCRAPS
STOOL

Tools

PENCIL
SCISSORS
MOD PODGE CRAFT GLUE
FOAM PAD BRUSH
X-ACTO KNIFE
WALLPAPER BRUSH OR
  BURNISHING TOOL
MEASURING TAPE (OPTIONAL)

How-To

1. Place the wallpaper pattern-side down on your work surface.

2. Set the stool upside down on the paper.

3. Trace around the top of the stool with a pencil.

4. Cut out the circle with scissors.

5. With the stool right-side up, brush the seat with a layer of Mod Podge.

6. Carefully place the paper onto the seat, and use your X-Acto knife to cut off any excess paper from around the edges.

7. Use a wallpaper brush or burnishing tool to smooth the paper and remove any air bubbles.

8. Cover the surface with a layer of Mod Podge, and set the stool aside to dry.

9. Seal and protect your paper with two to three additional coats of Mod Podge.

10. To cover the insides of the legs, use a measuring tape to get the dimensions, then cut out the appropriate-size strips of paper. Adhere them to the legs just as you did for the top surface (steps 6 through 9 above).

We're not ashamed to admit that we've eaten our fair share of meals off of TV trays. We love them for their casual convenience, but do our best to stash them out of sight when company comes around. These, on the other hand, cleaned up so nice with so little effort, we think it's about time to organize our first TV dinner party.

Materials

FOLDING TV TRAY
WALLPAPER SCRAPS
CLEAR CONTACT PAPER

Tools

SPRAY PAINT (OPTIONAL)
METAL RULER
PENCIL
X-ACTO KNIFE
SPRAY ADHESIVE
BONE FOLDER OR
   BURNISHING TOOL

How-To

1. Spruce up an old tray with a coat or two of spray paint. Set it aside to dry.

2. Measure the dimensions of the tray top, and draw the measurements on the back side of your wallpaper with a pencil and ruler.

3. Cut out the piece of wallpaper with an X-Acto knife, using a metal ruler as your guide.

4. Apply a layer of spray adhesive to the back side of the wallpaper.

5. Carefully set the paper in place on your tray top, and use a bone folder or burnishing tool to smooth out any bubbles.

6. To protect and seal the wallpaper, measure and cut out a piece of clear contact paper the same size as your tray top.

7. Peel off the backing and place the contact paper over the wallpaper. Smooth out any bubbles with a bone folder or burnishing tool.

Glass-covered Side Table

CREATE A SWAPPABLE SURFACE FOR EVERY OCCASION.

Change is good. We change the clothes we wear and the foods we eat, but when it comes to furniture, when you pick something up you're pretty much stuck with it—which is what makes the idea of a customizable table so appealing. This project allows you to switch it up based on the season, a particular occasion, or even your mood.

Materials

TABLE
WALLPAPER SCRAPS
GLASS TOP

Tools

METAL RULER OR
   MEASURING TAPE
PENCIL
UTILITY KNIFE

How-To

1. Measure the surface you plan to cover with a ruler or measuring tape.

2. Transfer the measurements onto the back side of your wallpaper, and cut out your new tabletop using a utility knife and a metal ruler as your guide.

3. Have a local glass shop cut you a piece using the same measurements. Make sure they grind, or "swipe," the edges so you can safely handle the glass when cleaning or swapping out different papers.

4. Set your paper onto the tabletop and place the glass on top of it, making sure not to bend or crease the paper. No adhesive is necessary.

Window Shade

AN EXCITING ALTERNATIVE TO NORMALLY BLAND BLINDS.

With its vertically oriented design, wallpaper is the perfect candidate for cut-and-fold window dressings. It's not only a great way to showcase your favorite paper, it will keep all your nosy neighbors at bay.

Materials

WALLPAPER SCRAPS
    (ENOUGH TO FIT YOUR
    WINDOW PLUS 24")
⅜" SQUARE WOODEN DOWEL
STRING OR COTTON YARN
2 SMALL HOOKS AND EYES

Tools

RULER OR MEASURING TAPE
PENCIL
SCISSORS OR UTILITY KNIFE
SMALL HOLE PUNCH
TACKY GLUE
BLUE PAINTER'S TAPE OR
    CLAMPS (OPTIONAL)
DREMEL (OPTIONAL, TO PRE-
    DRILL HOLES FOR HOOKS
    AND EYES)

Tip

To raise the shade, gather up the pleats to your desired height and secure each side with a paper clip—either over the folded paper or through each string underneath the folds.

How-To

1. Measure the length and width of your window. Subtract ½" from the width and add an extra 24" to the length.

2. Draw this measurement on your wallpaper and cut it out using scissors or a utility knife.

3. Fold the paper accordion-style, from top to bottom, with 2" between each fold.

4. Punch two small holes in each 2" panel for the string, 1" from the left edge of the paper and 1" from the right edge.

5. Cut your dowel to match the width of your paper.

6. Apply a thin bead of glue down all four sides of the dowel and wrap the top edge of the folded paper around all four sides. You may want to secure the paper to the dowel with blue painter's tape or clamps until the glue dries.

7. Thread two lengths of string or cotton yarn through the holes on both sides of the paper, and tie a knot at the top and bottom of each.

8. Screw in the eyes 2" from either end of the dowel, and use these to mark the placement of the hooks on the top of your window frame. If necessary, drill these holes in the dowel with a Dremel tool.

9. Screw in the hooks and suspend the window shade. Once the shade is in place, you can determine if the length is a good fit for your window. Trim off any excess paper, making sure not to cut the strings.

Room Divider

A STUNNING WAY TO SPLIT UP YOUR SPACE.

Whether you're looking for a little extra privacy, or you want to create a whole room-within-a-room, setting up a couple of bi-fold doors is a great place to start. Covering the panels in paper will make them blend into their surroundings and prevent them from looking like someone dropped a cubicle in your living room.

Materials

BI-FOLD DOORS

WALLPAPER (1 TO 2 ROLLS, DEPENDING ON THE SIZE AND NUMBER OF BI-FOLD DOORS)

Tools

MEASURING TAPE

PENCIL

METAL RULER OR CARPENTER SQUARE

UTILITY KNIFE

PAINT (OPTIONAL)

WALLPAPER PASTE AND BRUSH

PLASTIC FLOAT

SCREWDRIVER (OPTIONAL)

How-To

1. Measure the doors and cut your paper to size using a utility knife and metal ruler or carpenter square as your guide, leaving a 2" allowance on the top and bottom.

2. If you would like the sides of the dividers to match the paper, paint the edges of the doors in a complementary color and let them dry completely.

3. Apply paste and book your wallpaper (see page 19 in Wallpaper 101 for more on this technique).

4. Carefully place your wallpaper on the first room divider door.

5. Smooth down the paper with a brush and remove any air bubbles with a plastic float.

6. Trim off the excess paper at the top and bottom using a utility knife.

7. Repeat for the other door, matching up the pattern.

Tip

If you are creating a wider room divider using multiple bi-fold doors, attach them together using the provided hinge.

Interior Door Panel

ADD AN ELEMENT OF SURPRISE TO A DÉCOR-DEPRIVED SPOT IN YOUR HOME.

The last time we decorated a door we were in junior high, and believe us, it wasn't pretty. But with their vertical, unadorned faces, doors offer an irresistible blank canvas for wallpaper. Regardless of what paper you choose, it's guaranteed to look better than that New Kids on the Block collage did.

Materials

WALLPAPER

Tools

MEASURING TAPE

PENCIL

UTILITY KNIFE

METAL RULER

WALLPAPER PASTE AND BRUSH

PLASTIC FLOAT

SPONGE

How-To

1. Measure the interior of your door and transfer the measurements to the back side of your wallpaper.

2. Cut out the paper for your door panel using a utility knife and metal ruler as your guide.

3. Apply paste to the wallpaper, and adhere it to your door.

4. Smooth down the paper with a brush and remove any air bubbles with a plastic float.

5. Wipe off any excess paste with a damp sponge.

Staircase

A STEP-BY-STEP WAY TO CREATE A HEAVENLY STAIRWAY.

Outside of casinos and cruise ships, you don't see too many ornately decorated staircases these days. Which is too bad. We're not advocating lining your steps with Technicolor industrial carpeting, we just think this might be a missed opportunity. Papering the risers of even the most modest staircases can make them look grand.

Materials

WALLPAPER

Tools

MEASURING TAPE
METAL RULER
PENCIL
UTILITY KNIFE
WALLPAPER PASTE AND BRUSH
PLASTIC FLOAT
SPONGE
BROAD KNIFE

How-To

1. Carefully measure the stair risers (the vertical surface between the stairs) and cut your paper to size. If you want the pattern to line up along the length of the staircase, you will want to make your cuts as precise as possible. Take a good look at each step and take note of any bowing before making your cut.

2. Prepare and book your wallpaper, and apply as you would to the wall (see page 19 in Wallpaper 101 for more on this technique).

Switch Plate Cover

ARTFULLY DISPLAY (OR DISGUISE) YOUR SWITCH PLATE OR OUTLET.

Whether you want to draw attention to your switch plates or camouflage them with surrounding paper, covering one with wallpaper is a small design gesture that can make a great impact on a room.

Materials

SWITCH PLATE AND SCREWS
WALLPAPER SCRAPS
   (APPROXIMATELY 6" SQUARE)

Tools

METAL RULER
X-ACTO KNIFE
PENCIL
SPRAY ADHESIVE

How-To

1. Cut a piece of your wallpaper at least 1" larger than your switch plate on all sides using an X-Acto knife and metal ruler as your guide.

2. Lay the paper pattern-side down on your work surface and place the switch plate in the center.

3. Trace the outline of the plate with a pencil.

4. Remove the plate and miter all four corners of the wallpaper at 45-degree angles. (For an example, see the corner cuts on page 59, Accordion-page Photo Album).

5. Apply an even layer of spray adhesive to the front of the switch plate and the back of the wallpaper.

6. Set the plate facedown on the wallpaper and press firmly.

7. Apply an even layer of adhesive to the plate backing.

8. Fold the sides of the paper over the back of the switch plate, followed by the top and bottom, and press into place.

9. Cut an "x" from the corners of the switch slot with an X-Acto knife, and fold the paper edges over the slot edges.

10. Place the plate over your light switch and attach with screws.

Headboard

PASTE UP A PRETTY FRAME FOR YOUR BED.

Since we've never found a headboard we were in love with, we spend an inordinate amount of time in the morning fluffing up our pillows to conceal as much of it as possible. Crafting one out of wallpaper opens up all kinds of possibilities: Not only can you play with colors and patterns, but you can cut out shapes as ornate or simple as you'd like.

Materials

LARGE PIECE OF SCRAP PAPER
    FOR TEMPLATE
WALLPAPER (SEE BED WIDTHS
    BELOW)

Tools

MEASURING TAPE
PENCIL
SCISSORS
BLUE PAINTER'S TAPE
    (OPTIONAL)
WALLPAPER PASTE
BRUSH OR PAINT ROLLER
PLASTIC FLOAT
SPONGE

How-To

1. Measure the width of your bed and decide how tall you want the headboard (see standard bed widths below).

2. To create a template, photocopy or trace our Headboard template on page 140 or draw your own template design on scrap paper. To ensure symmetry, make the template for one half of the headboard and flip it over so that it mirrors itself when tracing out your design.

3. Cut out the template from the scrap paper with scissors, and trace the design onto your wallpaper of choice. If your design is wider than two sheets of wallpaper, you may need to align and piece three sheets together. We suggest lining up the seams and temporarily taping them into one piece with blue painter's tape before tracing and cutting out your design.

4. Cut out your wallpaper headboard, and apply the paper to your wall as you would normal sheets of wallpaper (see Wallpaper 101 on page 19 for more on this technique).

Standard Bed Widths

Single: 39"
Double/Full: 54"
Queen: 60"
King: 76–78"
California King: 72"

Archway

CREATE A DYNAMIC DIVISION BETWEEN ROOMS.

A little paper goes a long way when it comes to accenting architectural details in your home. By lining the interior of an archway or door frame you can transform an otherwise unremarkable spot into something worth noticing.

Materials

WALLPAPER

Tools

MEASURING TAPE
PENCIL
UTILITY KNIFE
WALLPAPER PASTE AND BRUSH
PLASTIC FLOAT
4" BROAD KNIFE

How-To

1. Measure the length and width of the arch and cut your wallpaper to size, leaving an extra 2" on each end.

2. Paste and book your wallpaper (see page 19 in Wallpaper 101 for more on this technique).

3. Start at the top of the first wall and smooth the paper down to the floor, with the extra 2" at the bottom.

4. Press the paper snugly into the top corner, smooth it across the arch, press it into the opposite corner, and smooth it down to the floor. You should have 2" extra at the bottom.

5. Smooth down the paper with a brush and remove any bubbles with a plastic float.

6. Once the paper has set, use the broad knife and utility knife to remove excess paper from the bottom edges.

Framed Wallpaper Art

PAPER SO PRETTY IT BELONGS IN A FRAME.

Sometimes even just a hint of wallpaper can liven up a room. Whether you're commitment-phobic or you've just discovered a beautiful vintage scrap at the flea market, hanging your paper in a frame means small sections can be rearranged or removed at a moment's notice. Don't like the way the paper looks in your bedroom? Hang it in the kitchen instead.

Materials

ASSORTED PICTURE FRAMES

WALLPAPER SCRAPS (ENOUGH
   TO FIT FRAMES)

HANGING HARDWARE
   (OPTIONAL)

Tools

METAL RULER

X-ACTO KNIFE

SPRAY PAINT

How-To

1. Based on the size of your frames, measure and cut out your wallpaper scraps using an X-Acto knife and metal ruler as your guide.

2. Spray paint the frames a complementary color, and set them aside to dry.

3. Insert your paper into the frames and hang them on a wall, or arrange them along a decorative ledge.

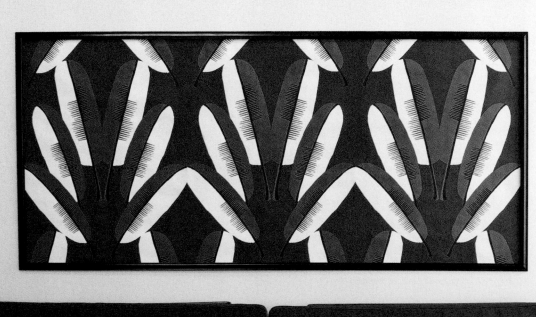

Wallpaper Framed with Molding

FABRICATE AN OVERSIZED FRAME WITH AN INEXPENSIVE HARDWARE STORE STAPLE.

There's no rule that says wallpaper must cover an entire wall. It's up to you to decide how much or how little to use. Creating a custom frame from molding is an artful and affordable way to highlight a special area or object in a room.

Materials

MOLDING

WALLPAPER

Tools

MEASURING TAPE

METAL RULER OR
   CARPENTER SQUARE

PENCIL

MITER OR CHOPSAW

PAINT OR STAIN

UTILITY KNIFE

LEVEL

WALLPAPER PASTE AND BRUSH

PLASTIC FLOAT

SPONGE

NAILGUN (OR A HAMMER
   AND FINISHING NAILS)

How-To

1. Measure the space you want to cover with wallpaper, and draw the perimeter lightly on the wall with a pencil.

2. Measure the molding and cut it to size with a miter or chopsaw, so the inside edge of the frame overlaps your wallpaper by about ¼".

3. Paint or stain the molding, and set it aside to dry.

4. Measure and cut your wallpaper to size, and apply it to the wall (see Wallpaper 101 on page 18 for more on this technique).

5. Frame the wallpaper with the molding by attaching it to the wall with a nailgun, or a hammer and finishing nails.

Framed Paper in Different Colorways

PLAY AROUND WITH MULTIPLE VERSIONS OF THE SAME PATTERN.

Picking a wallpaper can be as exhausting as it is exhilarating. So many styles, patterns, and motifs to choose from! And once you've finally settled on a style you love, it will most likely come in three or four different colorways, any number of which would look great in your home. However, with a little strategizing you can have the best of all worlds: Turn smaller pieces of your runner-up paper into framed wall art, and hang them against your primary paper, lining up the patterns to match what's on your wall.

Materials

PRIMARY WALLPAPER
(1 TO 2 ROLLS WILL COVER
A MODEST-SIZED WALL)
SECONDARY WALLPAPER IN
DIFFERENT COLORWAY
PICTURE FRAMES WITH
HANGING HARDWARE

Tools

WALLPAPER PASTE AND BRUSH
PLASTIC FLOAT
BLUE PAINTER'S TAPE
PENCIL
SPONGE
BROAD KNIFE
UTILITY KNIFE

How-To

1. Apply paste and hang your primary wallpaper, if it isn't already installed (see Wallpaper 101 on page 17 for more on this technique).

2. Use blue painter's tape to temporarily tack up a sheet of the secondary paper where you want to place the frame, making sure to match up the pattern with the primary paper.

3. Hold the frame backing up on the wall and trace around it with a pencil.

4. Remove the secondary paper from the wall, cut out your piece, and insert it into the frame.

5. Use the hanging hardware to carefully place the frame in position over the primary paper.

Wall Letters

ADD DEPTH TO ANY WALL WITH A THREE-DIMENSIONAL MONOGRAM.

Decorating with letters is a fun and easy way to personalize your space. Hanging a few here and there or spelling out entire words can be a beautiful way to make a bold statement or simply set the mood.

Materials

CARDBOARD OR WOOD
LETTERS (AVAILABLE
AT CRAFT STORES)
WALLPAPER SCRAPS

Tools

PENCIL
SCISSORS
RUBBER CEMENT

How-To

1. Place the letters face up on the front of your wallpaper.

2. Lightly trace around the edges with a pencil.

3. Cut out your shapes with scissors.

4. Apply a layer of rubber cement to the back of the wallpaper and the surface of the letters.

5. Smooth down the paper over the letters.

Swatch Watch

Try this project with **A.** a bright floral, **B.** a bold geometric, or **C.** a striking oversized print.
See Resources on page 142 for details.

A.

B.

C.

Silhouette Art

CREATE A CLASSIC PORTRAIT OF SOMEONE SPECIAL IN YOUR LIFE.

Commissioning a traditional portrait is a time-honored way of paying tribute to the most important and beloved member of the household. Creating your own *un*traditional portrait is much more fun and still gets the point across.

Materials

WALLPAPER SCRAPS IN TWO
    COMPLEMENTARY COLORS
FRAME
SCRAP PAPER FOR TEMPLATE
    (OPTIONAL)

Tools

SPRAY PAINT
PENCIL
SCISSORS
X-ACTO KNIFE
RUBBER CEMENT

How-To

1. Choose your wallpapers.

2. Remove the glass and backing from the frame. Spray paint the frame to match your wallpapers and let it dry completely.

3. Photocopy or trace our Dog Silhouette template on page 139 onto scrap paper, or come up with your own design. Trace it in reverse on the back side of one of your wallpaper scraps. To avoid wasting your wallpaper, you may want to first test the fit in the frame with a template made of scrap paper.

4. Cut out your silhouette with scissors or an X-Acto knife.

5. Place the frame facedown on the background paper.

6. Trace around the interior of the frame with a pencil and cut out the paper.

7. Apply an even layer of rubber cement onto the back of the silhouette and the front contact area of the background paper, and press them together.

8. Reassemble the frame with your new artwork.

Cutout Wallpaper Shapes

CREATE A SCENE WITH ONE-OF-A-KIND WALL DECALS.

Wallpaper offers endless ways to inject playfulness and personality into a room. Forget about plumb lines and matching seams for the moment, and cut out all sorts of crazy shapes and motifs instead.

Materials

WALLPAPER SCRAPS

Tools

PENCIL
SCISSORS OR X-ACTO KNIFE
WALLPAPER PASTE AND
 BRUSH OR PAINT ROLLER
PLASTIC FLOAT
SPONGE

How-To

1. Draw your design in reverse on the back side of your wallpaper.

2. Cut out the shape with scissors or an X-Acto knife.

3. Apply wallpaper paste and hang your cutout shape just as you would a regular sheet of wallpaper (see Wallpaper 101 on page 19 for more on this technique).

Swatch Watch

Try this project with **A.** a printed grasscloth, **B.** a retro graphic, or **C.** a kaleidoscopic floral.
See Resources on page 142 for details.

A.

B.

C.

Layered Cutouts

CUT AND PASTE A WALLPAPER COLLAGE.

With so many great wallpaper options available today, choosing just one can be a stressful ordeal. One may be the perfect color, but maybe you're in love with another's particular motif. Why choose at all when you can so easily have both?

Materials

WALLPAPER
(TWO COMPLEMENTARY
PATTERNS, PREFERABLY
ONE LARGE-SCALE PRINT
AND ONE SMALL)

Tools

WALLPAPER PASTE AND BRUSH
PLASTIC FLOAT
SPONGE
SCISSORS

How-To

1. Apply paste and hang your primary paper, if it isn't already installed (see Wallpaper 101 on page 17 for more on this technique).

2. Cut out your desired shapes from the secondary paper.

3. Apply paste on the back side of the secondary paper and adhere it to the wall.

4. Smooth down the cut-out shapes with a brush and remove any air bubbles with a plastic float.

5. Wipe off any excess paste with a damp sponge.

Tip

Special pastes, such as vinyl-on-vinyl paste for wallpaper borders, are perfect for projects like this.

Stripes of Wallpaper and Paint

SOMETIMES TWO TECHNIQUES ARE BETTER THAN ONE.

Though many people often think of it as an "either/or" situation, there's no reason wallpaper and paint can't share a wall. It's not only a great way to highlight a particular color from a pattern, but you'll get a lot more mileage out of every roll.

Materials

WALLPAPER
PAINT

Tools

PAINT TRAY AND ROLLERS
DROP CLOTH FOR PAINTING
MEASURING TAPE
UTILITY KNIFE
METAL RULER
PENCIL
LEVEL
WALLPAPER PASTE AND BRUSH
PLASTIC FLOAT
SPONGE

How-To

1. Most wallpaper is printed with a design larger than you will want for your wall stripe. Choose a simple pattern, or one with a motif that lends itself to a slender 6" to 8" strip.

2. Take a swatch of your wallpaper to a paint supply store and find a complementary paint color.

3. Prep and paint your walls. Let them dry overnight.

4. Measure the height of your walls and cut out your wallpaper strips to size using a utility knife and a metal ruler as your guide.

5. Use a pencil and ruler to mark where you will place the strips of wallpaper.

6. Apply paste on the back side of the wallpaper, book the strips, and adhere them to the walls, using the marks as guides (see Wallpaper 101 on page 19 for more on this technique).

7. Once you've pasted up all the wallpaper pieces, go over each strip again with the plastic float to make sure the edges are perfectly flush with the wall.

8. Apply more paste as necessary and wipe off any excess paste with a damp sponge.

Wallpaper Patchwork

MIX AND MATCH FAVORITE PATTERNS TO CREATE A COLORFUL GRID.

When collecting wallpaper samples for a project, you may find that certain papers go particularly well together. Sometimes they look even better as a group than they do on their own. Patch a variety of pieces together to create a vibrant collage of complementary patterns and colors.

Materials

WALLPAPER SAMPLES
   OR SCRAPS

Tools

UTILITY KNIFE
METAL RULER
PENCIL
LEVEL
WALLPAPER PASTE AND BRUSH
PLASTIC FLOAT
SPONGE

How-To

1. Collect a number of different papers you would like to patch-work together. Look for interesting combinations of both color and pattern. Be sure to read the labels of the various papers, as some may require different methods of application (for example, prepasted versus unpasted, vinyl versus paper, and so on).

2. Choose a size for your patchwork, and cut all your samples to the same dimension (our squares are 9") using a utility knife and metal ruler as your guide.

3. Lay the pieces out on the floor and arrange them in a pattern you are happy with.

4. Using a pencil and ruler, mark out guides on the wall where the patchwork will go.

5. Apply paste to the back sides your wallpaper squares and adhere them to the wall (see Wallpaper 101 on page 19 for more on this technique). Start with a central row and work your way out to either side.

6. Wipe off any excess paste with a damp sponge.

sugar is thoroughly dissolved and mixture is frothy and foamy. Stir in Sherry. Pour into large glass punch bowl. In small deep bowl, combine the ½ cup cold water, lemon juice and ½ cup nonfat dry milk. Whip at high speed in electric mixer 6 to 8 minutes, or until stiff. Drop by spoonfuls on top of milk-wine mixture. If desired, sprinkle lightly with nutmeg.

Sherried Apple Eggnog
(About 12 4-oz. servings)

Call this frothy mixture perfect for an evening refreshment, or perhaps as a light dessert after a satisfying luncheon. To give extra tang, add about 2 tablespoons lemon juice.

    3 eggs, separated
    ½ cup sifted powdered sugar
    ¼ teaspoon nutmeg
      Pinch salt
    2 cups California Sherry, chilled
    2 cups apple juice, chilled
    1 cup heavy cream

Beat egg yolks with half of the sugar, nutmeg and salt until thick and lemon colored. Stir in chilled California Sherry and apple juice. Beat egg whites to soft peaks; add remainder of the sugar gradually continuing to beat until stiff meringue forms. Fold into chilled Sherry and egg yolk mixture; fold in cream, whipped until stiff. Serve in cups, with a light sprinkle of nutmeg. Accompany with a teaspoon.

---

container for a large amount of cold beverage from an out-size mixing or salad bowl. Set the bowl in a wreath of greens, with perhaps a few floaters. Freeze a fruit block or ring to float in the punch.

Frosty Orange Cooler
(1 serving)

Delightful to serve from its own orange shell container is this cool and refreshing drink.

    ½ cup California Dry Sherry, chilled
    ½ cup orange juice, chilled
    1 tablespoon each honey and lemon juice
    1 drop mint extract
    1 cup crushed ice

Place all ingredients in blender and whirl to frappé consistency. Fill into orange shell and garnish with mint leaves. Serve with straw.

Vermouth Frost
(1 serving)

For that special person who loves daiquiris, here's a way to make the cold drink with an added flavor of California Dry Vermouth.

    ¼ cup (2-oz.) California Dry Vermouth
    2 tablespoons frozen daiquiri mix
    ½ cup crushed ice

Place all ingredients in blender and blend briefly, about 10 seconds. Serve at once in chilled glass.

Golden Dressing
(About ¾ cup)

Use this dressing for mixed vegetables, coleslaw or sliced cucumbers. For deeper golden color, increase the prepared mustard content to 2 teaspoons.

    ⅓ cup California Medium Sherry
    ¼ cup each dairy sour cream, mayonnaise
    2 tablespoons sweet pickle juice
    ½ teaspoon prepared mustard
    ¼ teaspoon each salt, paprika
    ½ teaspoon mustard seed

Combine all ingredients and beat well; chill to blend flavors.

Fruit-flavored Salad Dressing: Mash or sieve 1 cup apricots; stir in ¼ cup California Sherry and a tablespoon lemon juice. Beat in 2 tablespoons mayonnaise and fold in 1 cup heavy cream, beaten stiff. A speck of salt and a drop of almond extract rounds out the flavors. You'll find this an excellent dressing on fresh or canned fruit salads.

Pimiento Cheese Salad Dressing
(About 1 cup)

Use this dressing over hearts of lettuce or with any fruit or vegetable salad that takes kindly to a cheese flavor. With a fork, mash 1 (3-oz.) package pimiento cheese; gradually blend in ⅓ cup salad oil, 2 tablespoons lemon juice and ¼ cup California Medium Sherry, beating until mixture is smooth. Add 2 tablespoons chopped parsley, ½ teaspoon Worcestershire sauce and ¼ teaspoon each onion and garlic salts; mix well.

Apricot Sherry Dressing
(About 1 cup)

Here is a dressing that is golden and beautiful to serve with fruit and cottage cheese salad. Blend ½ cup apricot preserves with ¼ cup California Medium Sherry. Slowly beat in 1 tablespoon lemon juice, 3 tablespoons salad oil and ¼ teaspoon powdered ginger. Pour into container, cover and chill.

Easy Spinach Soufflé
(6 servings)

Don't let soufflés frighten you, just depend on this carefully tested recipe to see you through. It is interesting because it has a small amount of biscuit mix to help keep the soufflé elevated. A word of assurance, although soufflés do have to be served soon after they are baked, they will remain puffed up for 10 to 15 minutes if necessary.

    1 (12-oz.) package frozen chopped spinach,
      cooked according to directions on package
      or 1 cup chopped cooked fresh spinach
    ¾ cup milk
    ¼ cup biscuit mix
    ¼ cup California Dry Sherry
    ½ teaspoon nutmeg
    3 eggs, separated
    1 teaspoon salt
    ¼ teaspoon cream

Drain cooked sp[...] excess water. [...] cuit mix to ma[...] mainder of the [...] ture boils a[...] en egg yolks; [...] of tartar to [...] ach mixtu[...] or strai[...] bake in [...] until kn[...] at once f[...]

Broiled Tomatoes With Sherry. Tomatoes make a bright and delicious spot of interest on any luncheon or dinner plate. Cut medium large tomatoes crosswise into halves; pierce with fork and sprinkle generously with California Sherry. Season with salt, pepper and dried dill. Place under broiler for 5 to 7 minutes or until heated through. Combine equal parts mayonnaise and grated Cheddar cheese; put spoonful on each tomato, then return to broiler and brown lightly. Allow 1 to 2 halves per serving.

Green Beans in Cheese Sauce
(4 to 5 servings)

Green beans become much more important if they are served in a special smooth cheese sauce. Undiluted mushroom soup forms the basis of the sauce, then Parmesan cheese and a hint of white table wine such as California Sauterne or Chablis are added.

    1 (No. 2) can green beans, whole or cut
    ¼ cup California Dry Sauterne or other white table wine
    1 (10½-oz.) can condensed cream of mushroom soup,
      undiluted
    2 tablespoons grated Parmesan cheese

Drain liquid from beans; reserve liquid to use later in sauces and soups. In saucepan combine wine with undiluted mushroom soup and grated cheese; heat to boiling point, stirring constantly to smooth. Add beans; heat [...] serve in individual dishes. Be[...] uld be go[...] serve [...] with minute [...]

French Pork Birds
(6 servings)

[...]forting to know that although this [...] eniably homey, it is still good [...] company that might drop in. The [...] used in the sauce gives the pork [...] e. Scatter chopped chives, fresh

[...]der steaks, ¼ inch thick
[...] sage

Jelly and Wine for Pork Chops: Create extra-delicious pork chops by topping them, after browning, with a little quince, apple or currant jelly. Season as usual, then pour on ½ cup California Sherry for 6 chops. Cover tightly and simmer over low heat until meat is fork tender.

[...]pper and marjo[...] turn into bowl (re[...]spoons drippings in which to [...] and add toasted bread cubes, carrots, [...], beaten egg, bouillon, salt and pepper; mix well. Spread stuffing on pork steaks, roll meat up and tie with string; roll each in flour and brown birds [...] drippings. Place pork birds in 1½-quart casserole and add Sauterne. Cover and bake in moderate ov[...] (350°) for 1½ hours. (If desired, small carrots an[...] onions may be placed in the casserole about 45 min[...] utes before the meat is done.) To serve, remove [...] strings and arrange pork birds on platter, then p[...] some sauce from the casserole over them. Thi[...] sauce if it seems a little thin.

To accompany this dish: **California Medium o[...] terne or Rosé**

Wine Glazed Corned Pork
(8 to 10 servings)

This special glazed meat is handsome enough for your most important entertaining occasion. The pork cooks to an attractive pink, the glaze sparkles and the peaches add a sunny glow as they decorate the serving platter. Since it does take time to simmer the pork for the initial cooking, it's a good plan to do this the day before.

    1 7-pound leg corned pork, boned and tied
      Wine-Nectar Glaze
    1 or 2 (1-lb. 13-oz.) cans cling peach halves

Cover meat with cold water; bring to boil and skim. Cover and cook slowly until tender, about 2½ to 3½ hours. Cool meat in cooking liquid. Remove any fat from meat; place in shallow roasting pan. Spoon on some of the Wine Nectar Glaze and bake in moderate oven (375°) until hot and richly glazed, about 45 minutes. Baste meat frequently while cooking with remaining Wine Nectar Glaze.

During the last 15 minutes of baking, arrange drained cling peach halves in bottom of pan; spoon glaze on peaches and heat well. To serve, arrange Corned Pork on platter and surround with peach halves and green beans.

Wine Nectar Glaze

    3 tablespoons brown sugar
    ½ teaspoon dry mustard
    2 tablespoons wine vinegar
    ¾ cup apricot whole fruit nectar
    ¾ cup California Medium Sauterne
    1½ teaspoons instant minced onion
    2 teaspoons cornstarch

Combine all ingredients; bring to a boil before spooning over meat.

To accompany this dish: **California Chablis or Pinot Blanc**

APPETIZE[...]

Occasion[...] ularly w[...] mixture [...]

    1 (8-[...]
    ¼ cu[...]
    1 (6[...]
    3 tabl[...]
      otr[...]
    1 tea[...]
    1½ to [...]

In sauce[...] milk unt[...] Place ove[...] now and [...] chips or [...]

To ac[...] and Se[...]

Spicy wit[...] are a deli[...] fornia She[...] later in th[...] mix make[...] pastry.

    2 tab[...]
    4 tea[...]
    ½ cup[...]
    2 cups[...]
    ½ cup[...]
    1 (8½-[...]

In small [...] add onion[...] Sherry. Co[...] liquid is a[...] ing to bo[...] each piece[...] cooled rais[...] up from 1 [...] pinching en[...] sheet in n[...] until brow[...]

To acc[...] Sherry o[...]

chapterFOUR

DIY WALLPAPER ALTERNATIVES

Improvised Wallpaper

EXPLORE ALL SORTS OF EXCITING OPTIONS FOR PAPERING YOUR WALLS.

We normally advocate using "the right tool for the right job," but we also believe that rules were meant to be broken. Wallpaper from manufacturers is certainly easier to work with, more durable, and will give you gorgeous results, but sometimes you've got to try your own thing. So go crazy and try any paper that strikes your fancy.

Materials

MAPS

CHAIR RAIL

Tools

UTILITY KNIFE

PENCIL

METAL RULER

WALLPAPER PASTE AND BRUSH

PLASTIC FLOAT

SPONGE

MEASURING TAPE

CHOPSAW

PAINT OR STAIN

LEVEL

NAILGUN OR HAMMER AND
    FINISHING NAILS

Tip

You might want to try a test run in an out-of-the-way spot, like inside a closet or cabinet, before pasting up your wall. If it doesn't work out, check out page 25 for tips on removing wallpaper.

How-To

1. Gather up a nice collection of maps, recipe pages, or another paper you like.

2. Cut off any extraneous (or unattractive) bits, such as indexes, keys, or advertisements.

3. Mark the area on your wall that you plan to cover, and assemble or cut your paper to size.

4. Prep and apply wallpaper paste to the back sides of your paper. Note: Since they aren't intended to be used as wallpaper, the maps should be handled with care. If over-pasted they can rip, and if over-handled they can stretch and distort.

5. Smooth the paper along the wall with a brush and plastic float. A little bubbling is expected, especially along the maps' fold lines. Gently lifting up the paper and re-smoothing will eliminate this problem. Wipe off any excess paste with a damp sponge.

6. Measure and cut your chair rail with a chopsaw.

7. Paint or stain it as desired, and let it dry completely.

8. Use a level to position the chair rail. Make sure it overlaps the top of your paper.

9. Attach it to the wall using a nail gun, or hammer and finishing nails.

Tiled Photo Mural

SCAN AND ENLARGE A FAVORITE PHOTO FOR CUSTOM DECORATING ON A GRAND SCALE.

Photographic wall murals can make a big decorative impact. If your home furnishings don't quite lend themselves to a wooded glen or lunar landscape backdrop, flip through your photo album for inspiration. A simple landscape or portrait that has special meaning for you is the ultimate way to personalize your space.

Materials

PHOTO

WHITE PRINTER PAPER

Tools

SCANNER

PHOTO-EDITING SOFTWARE
  (SUCH AS ADOBE
  PHOTOSHOP)

SOFTWARE WITH PAGE-TILING
  PRINT OPTION (SUCH AS
  ADOBE ILLUSTRATOR)

PRINTER

X-ACTO KNIFE

LEVEL

PENCIL

WALLPAPER PASTE

PAINT ROLLER

PLASTIC FLOAT

SPONGE

Tip

If you don't have access to the software necessary to create a tiled wall mural, look to the Web for online resources, such as the Rasterbator (http://homo kaasu.org/rasterbator).

How-To

1. Choose a favorite snapshot and scan it at a high resolution, such as 1200 dpi—the higher the resolution, the less pixilated it will be when you enlarge it. You can also use a preexisting high-resolution digital photo.

2. Determine the dimensions for your mural and change the image size of your photo accordingly. Lower the resolution to 150 dpi so the size of your file doesn't get too large.

3. Open your photo in Adobe Illustrator, and choose "Tile Image-able Area" from the "Print" menu. A small preview of the pages to be printed will appear.

4. Print out the pages and trim off the white borders with an X-Acto knife, making sure to keep them in order. Lay out the pages in order and, if it helps, number them.

5. Draw a plumb line down the center of the wall area you plan to cover using a level and a pencil.

6. Apply a thin, even layer of wallpaper paste to the wall with the paint roller—just to the right of the plumb line. The pasted area should be a little wider than the paper.

7. Begin applying pages to the wall, lining the left side up with the plumb pencil line and overlapping the seams a bit to avoid any space between the pages.

8. Smooth down the paper with a plastic float, and wipe off any excess paste on the front of the pages with a sponge.

9. Continue applying pages to the wall, working from the middle out, and smoothing gently with the plastic float. Air bubbles should disappear once the wallpaper paste dries.

Copied Patterns from Fabrics

TURN A FAVORITE FROCK OR FABRIC INTO A ONE-OF-A-KIND WALLPAPER.

Even with all the wonderful designers and manufacturers out there, your dream wallpaper might be as close as your bedroom closet. Patterned textiles are an obvious and exciting option when it comes to covering your walls. Go bold with a favorite argyle, or choose a fancy floral print—the possibilities are as wide open as your wardrobe.

Materials

A FAVORITE FABRIC

WHITE PRINTER PAPER

Tools

COMPUTER WITH SCANNER

PRINTER

COLOR PHOTOCOPIER

LEVEL

PENCIL

METAL RULER

WALLPAPER PASTE AND BRUSH

PLASTIC FLOAT

SPONGE

How-To

1. Choose a favorite fabric to transform into wallpaper.

2. Scan the section of fabric that you want to serve as the "repeat" pattern in your wallpaper.

3. Print out the wallpaper on a printer, then make your color photocopies. (Obviously, the larger the paper size, the fewer pieces you'll have to print and paste on your wall.)

4. Apply paste to the wall and adhere the printouts using your plastic float to smooth out air bubbles as you go. Be sure to handle the pages with care as they are more prone to ripping or stretching than typical wallpaper.

Painted "Wallpaper"

WHEN WALLPAPER WON'T DO, FAKE IT WITH PAINT.

There are, of course, instances when wallpaper just isn't an option. If you're stuck with a blockheaded landlord or you just can't find the perfect paper, creating your own pattern in paint is a fantastic alternative. Whether you choose to paint freehand, or use a stencil or stamp, you can get the wallpaper look you want, and still manage to hold onto your security deposit.

Materials

PAINT

PLASTIC SHEET FOR STENCIL

Tools

X-ACTO KNIFE

RULER

LEVEL

PENCIL

BLUE PAINTER'S TAPE

PAPER PLATES (FOR PAINT
    PALETTES)

DROP CLOTH

FOAM STENCIL BRUSH
    (AVAILABLE IN CRAFT AND
    ART SUPPLY STORES)

PAPER TOWELS

PAINT PEN (OPTIONAL)

Alternative Application

Printing on the wall with a foam or rubber stamp is another easy and exciting way to create your own custom "paper." For a great example of this technique, flip to page 2.

How-To

1. Creating the "wallpaper look" with paint is all about pattern and repeat. Come up with a design you love (and can paint or stencil without driving yourself crazy), and decide how often and how far apart you want your repeats. The more you plan ahead, the less chance you have of screwing something up.

2. Cut out your stencil design in the plastic sheet with an X-Acto knife.

3. Use a ruler and a level to carefully plan out your pattern on a wall. You may want to lightly mark the locations of your design with a pencil and lay down the drop cloth before you start painting.

4. Once you've got It all mapped out, place your stencil against the wall and secure it with strips of blue painter's tape. It's important to keep your stencil flush against the wall so you get a crisp outline to your design.

5. Using a paper plate as your paint palette, dab some paint on your stencil brush and carefully apply it to the wall with dabs or "kiss" motions, making sure to cover the entire design. You don't want any paint to get underneath your stencil, so don't swipe or brush it on.

6. Carefully peel your stencil away from the wall, and wipe off any errant paint with a paper towel before continuing. You will inevitably get some paint underneath your stencil, so it's a good idea to check after every couple of applications.

7. Secure the stencil in the next spot with the painter's tape (recheck your measurements if necessary) and repeat. You can add details to your design, like the spines and stems on our leaf pattern, using a paint pen.

Project Templates

MINI WALLET A
enlarge 150 percent

CHECKBOOK TAB

MINI WALLET B
enlarge 150 percent

DOG SILHOUETTE
enlarge 400 percent

CLOCK
enlarge 200 percent

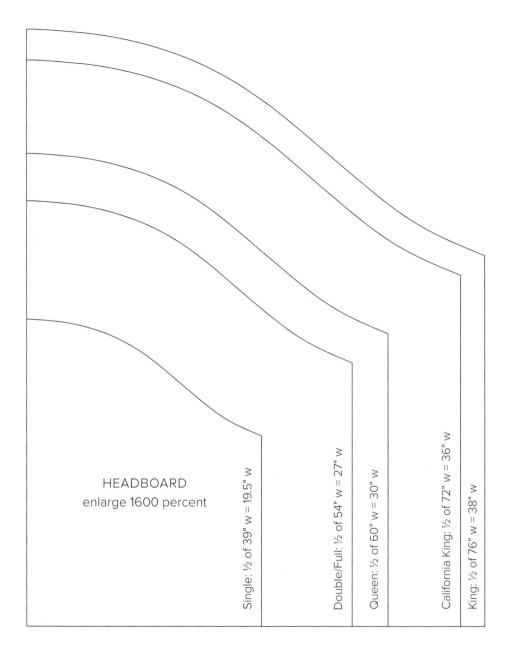

HEADBOARD
enlarge 1600 percent

Single: ½ of 39" w = 19.5" w

Double/Full: ½ of 54" w = 27" w

Queen: ½ of 60" w = 30" w

California King: ½ of 72" w = 36" w

King: ½ of 76" w = 38" w

To create your headboard, photocopy or trace this template, which is half the width of a complete headboard. Once you've copied the first half at the appropriate size, flip it over and copy or trace the other half to ensure symmetry.

Metric Conversion Chart

To convert inches into centimeters, multiply the measurement by 2.54.
All metric measurements in this chart have been rounded to the nearest tenth.

INCHES	CENTIMETERS	INCHES	CENTIMETERS
⅛	.32	15	38.1
¼	.64	15 ½	39.4
½	1.3	16	40.6
1	2.5	16 ½	41.9
1 ½	3.8	17	43.2
2	5.1	17 ½	44.5
2 ½	6.4	18	45.7
3	7.6	18 ½	47
3 ½	8.9	19	48.3
4	10.2	19 ½	49.5
4 ½	11.4	20	50.8
5	12.7	20 ½	52.1
5 ½	14	21	53.3
6	15.2	21 ½	54.6
6 ½	16.5	22	55.9
7	17.8	22 ½	57.2
7 ½	19	23	58.4
8	20.3	23 ½	59.7
8 ½	21.6	24	61
9	22.9	24 ½	62.2
9 ½	24.1	25	63.5
10	25.4	25 ½	64.8
10 ½	26.7	26	66
11	27.9	26 ½	67.3
11 ½	29.2	27	68.6
12	30.5	27 ½	69.9
12 ½	31.8	28	71.1
13	33	28 ½	72.4
13 ½	34.3	29	73.7
14	35.6	29 ½	74.9
14 ½	36.8	30	76.2

Wallpaper Index

Resources

NEW DESIGNS

2JANE: www.2jane.com, 877.252.6316 (distributors of Mibo and Wallpaper-by-Numbers)

ATA DESIGNS: www.atadesigns.com, +44 (0) 208 223 7263

BRADBURY & BRADBURY: www.bradbury.com, 707.746.1900

CAVERN: www.cavernhome.com, 310.694.8384 or 718.766.5464

COLE AND SON: www.cole-and-son.com, +44 (0) 207 376 4628

ERICA WAKERLY: www.printpattern.com, +44 (0) 7940 577 620

F. SCHUMACHER: www.fsco.com, 800.523.1200

FARROW & BALL: www.farrow-ball.com, 888.511.1121

FERM LIVING: www.ferm-living.com, www.fermlivingshop.us, 415.318.6412

FLAVOR PAPER: www.flavorleague.com, 504.944.0447

GRAHAM & BROWN: www.grahambrownusa.com, 800.554.0887

JILL MALEK: www.jillmalek.com, 718.207.9587

JONATHAN ADLER: www.jonathanadler.com, 800.963.0891

MOD GREEN POD: www.modgreenpod.com, 617.670.2000

NAKED & ANGRY: www.nakedandangry.com, 773.878.3557

NAMA ROCOCO: www.namarococo.com, 413.652.2312 (trade only)

ORLA KIELY: www.orlakiely.com (available at Anthropologie, www.anthropologie.com)

POTTOK: www.pottokprints.com, 323.666.1245

RAPTURE & WRIGHT: www.raptureandwright.co.uk, 01608 652442

ROLLOUT: www.rollout.ca, 604.681.3780

STUDIO NOMMO: www.studionommo.com, +90212 2934171

STUDIO PRINTWORKS: www.studioprintworks.com, 212.633.6727 or 201.795.9540

THIBAUT: www.thibautdesign.com, 800.223.0704

TIMOROUS BEASTIES: www.timorousbeasties.com, 00 44 (0)141 337 2622 or 00 44 (0)20 7833 5010

TROVE: www.troveline.com, 212.268.2046

TWENTY2: www.twenty2.net, 888.222.3036

WALL COLLECTION: www.wallcollection.com

WALNUT PAPERS: www.walnutwallpaper.com, 323.932.9166

WANDRLUST: www.wandrlust.com, 888.963.LUST

VINTAGE

EBAY.COM

ETSY.COM

SECONDHAND ROSE: www.secondhandrose.com, 212.393.9002

Index